TECHNOLOGY
LONGEVITY
ECONOMY
LIBERTY

Technology, Longevity, Economy, Liberty by Robert Ennis

© 2017 by Robert Ennis. All rights reserved.
No portion of this book may be reproduced in any form without
permission from the author, except as permitted by U.S. copyright law.
For permissions contact: bob.ennis@juno.com
Editing by: Hana Haatainen-Caye
Cover and Interior Design: Gabriela Carnabuci
ISBN: 978-1-387-01134-6
First Edition
Printed in The United States of America

TECHNOLOGY
LONGEVITY
ECONOMY
LIBERTY

ROBERT ENNIS

CONTENTS

PREFACE. i
INTRODUCTION We Have Gone Terribly Wrong. 1
CHAPTER 1 Poverty Amidst Plenty— Why? 19
CHAPTER 2 Industrial Technology and its Critics 33
CHAPTER 3 Information Technology and Automation 49
CHAPTER 4 Technology and Longevity 57
CHAPTER 5 War and Technology 63
CHAPTER 6 Economic Realities 69
CHAPTER 7 Political Failures and Polarization on Both Sides. . . 85
CHAPTER 8 The Failure of the Welfare State 95
CHAPTER 9 The Flawed Concept of "Free Trade" 103
CHAPTER 10 Drowning in Debt. 109
CHAPTER 11 Tackling the Triple Whammy 117
CHAPTER 12 There is a Sane Way Out 127
CHAPTER 13 Needed: Equities Market
Reforms to Retirements More Secure 145
CHAPTER 14 Dislodging Us From Dependency 165
CHAPTER 15 Closing Arguments 175
REFERENCES. 181
APPENDIX 1 Tackling the Debt 183
APPENDIX 2 Tackling the Trade Deficit 191
APPENDIX 3 Taming the Stock Market. 199

PREFACE

I began writing this book in 2015, around the time Donald Trump announced his decision to run for President. At the time, I considered his candidacy amusingly as I believed it would turn out to be a publicity stunt by someone who was prone to such stunts. Nevertheless, Trump started stating some things, certainly not all, that resonated with the themes I wanted to stress in my book about how our institutions were not keeping up with our technological realities and leaving many behind despite the general prosperity brought about by those realities. As his initial hyperbolic utterances were principally related to the unfettered unlawful migration of Hispanics across the southern border, it appeared that his flame would die out quickly.

Over time though, I noticed that he was saying things about the forgotten men and women whose status had been very much diminished by the loss of their well-paid manufacturing jobs in the industrial heartland. Now, that was a topic I could relate to. I had witnessed the huge migration to Texas of auto workers from Michigan and Ohio in the late '70s when plant after plant shut down because of the Japanese auto invasion. I saw the despair of workers in Pittsburgh in the early '80s when the loss of US auto manufacturing played its way upstream to the steel industry. I saw the results of huge losses of manufacturing even closer up in small town western Pennsylvania, once bustling with industrial activity now drying up as company after company shuttered and moved away.

So, when Trump began uttering his opposition to the trade deals that were at least partially responsible for this state of affairs, I sensed he was onto something, even as the media of both left and right were dismissing him. Unfortunately, these media moguls had fairly low regard for this group of displaced people. Yet, my experience had taught me that it was precisely this group who had paid an enormous price for the economic changes that have come into being since the advent of "Great Society" legislation, followed by the mass loss of high paid "breadwinner" employment as industry after industry fled overseas or to automation.

Then, to add insult to injury, the very same unfortunates who lost their jobs and middle class status over that period were reduced by the national media to racists, homophobes and misogynists. They "clung to their guns and religion." They were guilty of "white privilege." Well, maybe some were as bad as they were projected. Incendiary rhetoric began pouring out of the universities and elsewhere suggesting they were all beyond redemption. I saw it and I saw how many reacted. I would have reacted in a similar fashion. Then along came Trump and they had a spokesman. He rode that wave of despair to the White House and he has been accused of hate speech all along the way. I ask his accusers to look into the mirror and adjust to the new reality and admit that much of what has recently occurred is as much a result of their insensitivity to— if not outright hatred of—the typical heartland inhabitants they call rednecks or rubes or bible thumpers or any number of unflattering descriptions. Most are merely blue collar, white men, who have paid a heavy price for the economic changes that have occurred and who feel abandoned by the Democratic Party that now cares more about social issues than the bread and butter issues affecting not only them, but also blacks and Latinos at least as much.

Mr. Trump talked about the unfair trade deals that negatively impact the American worker and has pledged to reverse the damage it has caused by bringing back millions of jobs that have been lost to such unfair trade. I discuss that issue thoroughly. But he also talks of vast tax reductions without corresponding spending reductions and that is worrisome. Certainly, his call for a hiring freeze for non-essential federal employees is an idea I can embrace and is one way to reduce expenditures as is his pledge to roll back costly regulations in an effort to stimulate the economy. Nevertheless, a huge infrastructure bill, without paying for it, is not something I would support. More recently, his supporters talk about amortizing the cost over many years. That is an improvement of the concept but can only work if the infrastructure improvements he is considering are paid for by their users. Then bonds can be issued against them and the cost can be borne by the bondholders who can get a fair return on their investment in those improvements. Otherwise infrastructure spending will run up the debt even further than it is today and will add to our fiscal problems.

More important than anything else, he will have to come to grips with the negative tone he unleashed by his rhetoric. If he wishes to succeed, he will have to win the confidence of those who might even benefit from his economic ideas but were terrified by his inflammatory language. And, he will find out that much of his promised expenditures are far too costly to be carried out according to his poorly thought out plans. Yet, my sense is that his actions will conform to that reality because he is, first and foremost, a pragmatist as opposed to an ideologue and will change course if and when evidence shows that such change is necessary.

The problems of declining jobs for Americans and the ballooning debt have been around for a long time. I credit several authors, but David Stockman in particular, for informing me through their writing of how this has occurred. However, the possible solutions I discuss are altogether mine. I deserve whatever credit or blame my readers have for those.

I would like to thank my editor Hana Haatainen-Caye for her amazing efforts to clarify my writing. My lovely, highly talented granddaughter Gabriela Carnabuci laid out my manuscript and completed all activities associated with

Preface

bringing the book out. Finally, I am indebted to Gloria, my beautiful wife of over fifty years who, through numerous discussions, convinced me to see that both sides' conventional wisdom are mostly myths, are not workable, don't make any sense and probably never really did.

I believe that all of the solutions I propose in the book are workable. I have tried to be rigorous to ensure myself that the numbers work. But they are only a first step on the road to national solvency and greatness. I encourage all readers to weigh in and start a dialogue, recognizing that my proposals can certainly be improved on.

INTRODUCTION
WE HAVE GONE TERRIBLY WRONG

The fifties decade under Eisenhower was the golden age of U.S. prosperity. U.S. Steel and General Motors, as well as smaller versions of them, were flying high. In a period of what I call 'Corporate Socialism,' labor and management settled on decent wages and secure retirements for a generation of workers. Void of significant foreign competition, corporate management was able to pass along the cost of wage increases to the country as a whole. Union leaders were household names, more familiar than the heads of the very corporations with whom they negotiated.

The dollar was strong with the Swiss franc and German mark trading at about four to the dollar. The Japanese yen traded at 360 then. It hit 75, but currently has weakened to about 110 to the dollar.

Technology, Longevity, Economy, Liberty

In the mid-'60s, President Johnson fought the Vietnam War and the War on Poverty without funding either. This weakened the dollar by creating a cycle of deficit spending that funded the government. By 1971, the U.S. could no longer honor its long-standing obligation to pay its external debt with gold (at $35 an ounce). Essentially defaulting on this debt, President Nixon permitted the dollar to float, setting the stage for double digit inflation in the seventies and the rapid decline of the value of the dollar relative to other currencies. Nixon also embarked on a disastrous, short-lived wage and price freeze strategy. What was he thinking?

By 1980, the dollar had lost nearly half its value against the Japanese yen and similarly strong currencies. However, it still remained overvalued enough to allow the Japanese auto industry, propelled by its comparatively low wages, to penetrate the U.S. market with mostly low-end vehicles. Imports soared. The U.S. auto industry was ill prepared to match the still low prices, yet high quality, coming out of Japan, thus driving jobs in the automotive-related industries offshore. The era of the 'rust belt,' characterized by shut down factories and attendant unemployment, quickly emerged. Steel mills closed along Pittsburgh's Mon Valley, following the shuttering of numerous 'Big Three' auto plants.

At that time, my industry, the oil industry, was not affected. As a result of the weakened dollar, soaring oil prices created a boom in Texas and Oklahoma. But, for most of the country's middle class, the seventies represented a turn for the worse in the face of the emerging global economy. I was living in Houston then and witnessed the huge migration of rust belt workers pouring in. Many cars bore bumper stickers that read, *"Last one out of Michigan, shut off the lights."*

When I arrived in Pittsburgh to work for Dravo Engineers in 1982, the company was in a panic. The once proud Pittsburgh steel industry was in full retreat. The plight of all the displaced workers—first in Houston and then in Pittsburgh—never escaped me.

The same Nixon responsible for debasing our currency was also responsible for normalizing relations with China, but failed to receive much from them in return. Although he has been highly praised for this so-called accomplishment, I am not so sanguine. Since then, near slave labor has been producing our goods, steadily turning the U.S. into a debtor nation with far too many permanently unemployed or underemployed. The direct result? Our trillion-dollar-a-year deficit. Imagine what it would be like if the long-term unemployed were gainfully employed instead. The overtaxed federal budget would breathe a sigh of relief with Social Security and Medicare programs much less vulnerable.

The purpose of this book is to discuss this state of affairs. The so-called Global Economy has distorted our economy so much that it would be virtually unrecognizable to ordinary people only one generation ago. But it isn't the only significant change that has occurred. We are now faced with an unprecedented number of people living into their late '80s and beyond. Jobs are being replaced by machines at a breakneck pace. In my opinion, this is bringing us to an economic precipice. If we do not confront the problem soon, it

Technology, Longevity, Economy, Liberty

may be too late to reverse the trend. I fear we are, as a country, facing a similar decline experienced by other great nations.

I believe we need to understand the source of our problems if we are to have any chance of fixing them. I've written this book because I see no evidence, on both left and right that leads me to believe the political class has the knowledge, or the desire, to correct matters before it is too late. This book explains what I believe needs to be done, as well as undone.

In talking to people, I've found that both Democrats and Republicans, who may experience little common ground, agree that it is the understatement that we are not being governed well. It's possible, if an attempt is made, to bridge the gap between both sides' perceptions of where the problems lie.

As we let our guards down, it becomes clear we are speaking from the same malaise. If you are a Democrat, you're apt to defend runaway government spending, particularly where it applies to propping up the welfare of the poor. Yet, even so, you might question why so many people, close to a majority of the population, require such propping up. If, on the other hand, you are a Republican, you most certainly are asking the same question, along with some others. For example, if the Republicans are supposed to be the party of fiscal restraint, why were they so derelict in that responsibility during their governance, particularly during the presidencies of Nixon, Reagan, and George W. Bush? Or why did Vice President Cheney state that deficits no longer matter? Really?

We Have Gone Terribly Wrong

Regardless of your party affiliation, you may bemoan the fate of the once thriving middle class and question why only those well connected in big business and those who have access to government seats of power unavailable to the common man, have fared well in the advent of the global economy. Many have earned huge fortunes on Wall Street with super-sized leveraged speculation—in bubble after bubble—paying no price when the bubbles collapsed, because their enterprises were deemed "too big to fail."

You may not understand why collge tuition costs have gone through the roof while vocational training in high school has virtually vanished. Statistics show that approximately 40% of college students would have benefitted from such training, along with better guidance while in school. Both Democrats and Republicans are baffled by the consistent decline of able-bodied people in the work force while good-paying trade jobs are readily available. Have we mortgaged our industrial future to police states?

Naturally, we have our differences on social issues, but I question if they are really as insurmountable as our political elites would have us believe. For example, many on the right—most actually—do not begrudge same sex couples the same rights under the law as heterosexual couples. However, they do have an issue with calling their union a marriage. Why? Because they view marriage as a sacred bond, a religious one. They believe the line has been crossed regarding the separation of church and state, wondering why a compromise wasn't offered that could basically sidestep this issue. I could make a similar argument about other social issues. We *should* have more restrictive laws on late-term abortions. We *should not* allow firearms sales at gun shows without background checks.

So why is there so much polarization on these issues? I believe it is because our political elites and the media like it that way. A political class has taken over the country and remains intent on keeping the general population, the rabble, at bay by arguing among ourselves with relatively minor issues. The media of the political elites keeps us polarized even as the vast majority of us would like to put aside our differences on many petty divisive issues. We would like to return to a time when we had confidence that our government would solve our real problems rather than digging a deeper and deeper hole for our own, and future, generations.

The problem is critical. Consider the fact that five of the six wealthiest counties in the country are Washington, D.C. bedroom communities. Consider that in some of them, the average income for the top five percent is in excess of $500,000. That statistic alone should send shudders down the spine of every hard working American who is trying to play by the rules while so many in Washington peddle influence, pay for access, and alter the system in their favor.

The well-connected have distorted the system to such an extent that a large and growing sector of the country can barely make ends meet without appealing to the government. Eventually, as they grow more and more dependent, they become wards of the state and beholden to the government. That is a recipe for a future where many, if not all, have lost their liberty. It has happened before and will happen again.

We Have Gone Terribly Wrong

In my wildest imaginations as a youth, I never would have dreamt that my beloved country, the United States of America—the land that fought and defeated the Nazis and the Soviets—would succumb to an evil with the potential to be just as destructive. I have obsessed over these issues for quite a while, trying to understand its causes and cures. During that interval, countless images and thoughts have entered my mind.

The present state of affairs has not developed overnight. President Eisenhower warned us to beware of the Military Industrial Complex. We ignored him. President Johnson led us into a foreign war, Vietnam, and a domestic War on Poverty on a "Guns and Butter" policy, without paying for either. We yawned. The result of those fiscal improprieties led President Nixon to allow the dollar float and declare wage and price controls that led to a decade of double digit inflation and stagnation. We looked the other way, cheering when that same president "went to China," paving the way for the greatest loss in U.S. manufacturing jobs of all times. When President Reagan asked if we were better off with his policies, we nodded in affirmation, despite the government drowning in debt. And, after President Clinton and Speaker Gingrich finally created surpluses, President George W. Bush decided—with the blessing of Federal Reserve Chairman Greenspan—that tax cuts were more important than paying the country's bills with honest cash, resorting instead to overtime running of the printing presses. Then the final straw. We learned—many of us in disbelief—that President Obama could not manage the fiscal crisis thus created without racking up annual deficits of $1 trillion or higher.

Technology, Longevity, Economy, Liberty

As this came to pass, Republicans were "shocked, shocked" at the fiscal impropriety of this new administration. Their solution? Cut government spending. That would have been a laudable goal if the deficit were only bloated government spending alone. But the problem was also the result of tax cuts during President Bush's administration, much of which eased the burden on everybody, ordinary wage earners included. These cuts became sacrosanct as no Democratic administration would agree to raise taxes on these groups. Similarly, the mantra of Republicans since the Reagan years was uttered by President George W. Bush: "Read my lips. No new taxes."

The irresistible force met the immovable object. Now we're permanently stuck in the mud, each side blaming the other of intransigence, a perfect excuse by the political class to keep to business as usual. To hell with the people. Why not? By then, nearly half of the population was receiving government support, with more to come. The compliant populace was already compliant for a reason. Things could only get worse. If you are a net donor to this, you are perplexed. But you are among a shrinking majority on its way to being a minority. If you are a net recipient, even if you do not like your situation, you may reason that you have no choice. But, if you are a rent-seeking crony capitalist –with a distorted view that you are of the private sector—living large in one of those five overly wealthy D.C. suburbs while eating at the public trough, you will continue doing what you've been doing. After all, you somehow deserve your unearned wealth, right?

We Have Gone Terribly Wrong

That, my readers, is where I believe we are today. Good governance has gone out the window. The Democrats abandoned ship long ago. At least they had a reason, believing the ideology of the party. The Republicans had no such excuse. Their ideology was not intended to favor those who seek government relief as a means of prospering in the private sector. Now, things have reached new levels of concern. Big money in elections demands big donors. How can this be a good thing? And it only gets worse with each cycle. Of course, the system is prone to corruption and influence peddling, with both parties indulging. The general public is the victim.

Meanwhile, demographics, international finance, and longevity have exacerbated the problem further. In the 1950s, nobody would have imagined that the majority of vehicles we drive were not manufactured by the Big Three in Detroit. Nobody would have foreseen the demise of New York's garment district. Furniture, appliances, and television sets were all manufactured here at one time. Perhaps the loss of jobs to automation was inevitable, as were losses to foreign economies in a fair global marketplace. But what has happened is far more sinister. China, the world's largest police state, has manipulated its currency and kept its value so artificially low that it is nearly impossible for U.S. manufacturing to compete. Yes, our prices are low, but at what cost?

Just look at the U.S. national debt and trade balances since Nixon's fateful trip to China. Since then, we have imported over $8 trillion more than we have exported and participation of able-bodied workers in the work force has declined from about 80% of the potential workforce to about 62%. What has it accomplished? Imagine if that additional 18% were actually producing refrigerators, washing machines, TVs, sofas, dresses, suits, and Smartphones. Our GDP would be about $1 trillion greater and our deficit would totally disappear! We would be in surplus, even as an ever greater proportion of our population enters into retirement. Lower taxes would offset higher domestic prices. And our national self-esteem would be soaring rather than souring.

Our national debt has exploded since Nixon's trip to China. In 1972, the bleeding had barely begun, but it has grown completely out of proportion since then. **Here are the numbers:** [1]

YEAR	DEBT $ BILLION	GDP $ BILLION
1962	303	610
1972	436	1,294
1982	1,133	3,367
1992	4,002	6,587
2002	6,198	11,037
2012	16,050	16,228

Don't get me wrong; I do not begrudge the people of China or India or anywhere else to be beneficiaries of the great industrial revolution started right here in the U.S. It has spread to much of the rest of the world as technological innovation has continually reduced (inflation adjusted) prices for raw materials and finished goods. Of course, this is unrecognizable due to the mess our economists have made with the concept of currency. They inform us inflation is inevitable. If so, however, why was there zero inflation during all of the 19th century, when millions of poor immigrants flooded into the U.S. to participate in the economy that raised more people out of poverty than any other economy in the history of the world?

Indeed, the workers in the rest of the world are certainly entitled to the fruits of technology and of their labor. Why shouldn't the Chinese workers, who produce products for our consumption, have the wherewithal to enjoy those products for themselves? In many ways, these workers are even worse victims of the system.

It was most certainly an unintentional consequence, but the opening in China and the trade negotiations that ensued, created an atmosphere that allowed corrupt police state officials to be the principal beneficiaries. The wealthy, well-connected here also benefitted by obtaining an inexhaustible supply of cheap labor in China for their products while not losing the U.S. domestic market. What could possibly go wrong for the U.S. middle class factory worker? Against this background, I certainly understand his anger and cries against the one percent. A tiny fraction of the population of the country obtained tremendous wealth and power at his expense.

This background provides a clearer picture of the reason so many dropped out of the workforce. Perhaps they have made a rational decision to become a ward of the state rather than seek employment. Rather than condemning them, we should focus our condemnation on the policies and the people who have orchestrated the situation for their own benefit. And, we should recognize it and work to change it.

Technology, Longevity, Economy, Liberty

This book addresses these issues. I have attempted fairness to all sides, assessing blame where appropriate. But I am not neutral. I mainly fault the Republican establishment conservatives—the so-called believers in capitalism and free enterprise—who have made a mockery of the principles for which they ostensibly stand. I am not a fan of Reaganomics any more than I am a fan of the Nixon foreign policy and economic debacles. When you consider the ballooning debt during the Gipper's watch, you must conclude that much of the prosperity since his years in the White House came with the instability of debt financing.

Without all the accumulated indebtedness since Nixon let the dollar float and opened our economy to Chinese kleptocrats, no president, no matter how statist his predilections, would dare to run up such huge deficits as were accumulated under our last two highly unqualified Chief Executives. The numbers reveal that, despite posturing to the right, the George W. Bush years were as derelict of fiscal rectitude as the Obama years have been. That terrible truth will make it all the more difficult if and when a new crop of politicians, trying to reverse decades of Republican and Democrat malfeasance, get elected and grapple with getting things right. It will take decades, if it can be done at all. The damage will not be undone overnight.

These are the issues I discuss in this brief treatise. I have tried to eliminate as much jargon as possible, used only to convey the impression by the user that the subject is far too complex to be understood by the uninitiated. I believe that is baloney. If a subject cannot be explained so a person with ordinary education and cognitive skills can understand it, then the explainer probably does not know the fundamentals of his subject as well as he assumes he does. True knowledge clarifies issues; it doesn't obscure them. I have set out to write a book about these important issues from a layman's point of view. William Buckley once remarked that he would rather be governed by the first 100 people in the New Haven telephone directory than by the faculty of Yale. Likewise, George Orwell commented that some things are so unbelievable that only an intellectual could believe them. In my own experience, I have seen that too many people I consider quite intelligent are, nevertheless, not too smart.

In the beginning chapters of *Technology, Longevity, Economy, Liberty,* I discuss the benefits of technology and the failure of so-called experts who have warned us time after time that our industry led way of life will lead to disaster, only to have failed with their dire predictions. I discuss how these same experts, or their intellectual heirs, try to convince us of the unerring quality of their equally dire predictions for the future, doing everything in their power to stifle any opposition to the course they set. I also discuss a compliant media that echoes their directives and predictions. I challenge you, my readers, to think for yourselves, to "connect the dots" in order to understand exactly where these experts are leading them.

Early in the book, I lay out my thoughts as clearly as I can as to my understanding of what caused our economy to be so distorted and unstable. I take on the enemies of technology—those who have cried "wolf" so many times in the past with their warnings about the dangers of starvation and over-population that have not come to pass. I rail that they have not connected the dots to acknowledge that technology, borne of human ingenuity, has been the missing ingredient that has ultimately saved us from those dire predictions for the future. I call out these false prophets for what they are and bemoan that the Democrats—running a party I once called mine—have adopted their unwarranted warnings hook, line, and sinker and govern accordingly. Why am I calling out the Democrats? Simply because of their apparent belief that the government can pay its outlandish bills forever with freshly printed fiat money. I call them out for sticking to a welfare state model which has clearly failed. Every election cycle sees them blaming everyone but themselves for the shocking—and growing—level of dependency in the country as they demand even more money for failed programs and more classes of victims.

I also call out the solutions offered by the Republicans, particularly those in the long-standing establishment. Their remedies are far from reassuring. I don't blame intelligent people for being skeptical and distrustful. There is good reason that in the 2016 cycle, establishment candidates in both parties are being abandoned in favor of outsiders of the status quo who vow to take the party and the country in a new direction. The Democrats' answer is outright socialism. The Republicans' answer should be a rejection of the establishment leaders who appear to be more interested in retaining their jobs than creating a place where there is incentive for businesses to thrive right at home; a place where sound money is restored as the government slowly gets its finances into balance and, collectively, we produce as much as we consume.

We Have Gone Terribly Wrong

Attempting to wrap my mind around the national debt problem, I have examined the issue and have come to the conclusion that the debt will be around for a long time. But, even at relatively low growth, it can be paid down. It took nearly 50 years to get here, so it is madness to think we can get out of it quickly. The system has to be put on a course to correct itself gradually in order to avoid a major crash. My analysis addresses the modest and gradual reduction of discretionary spending and entitlement spending. Common sense reforms are desperately needed in order to transform our stock market from its position as a vast gambling casino to its primary function—a place where ordinary people can invest their money and earn a fair return based on the performance of the companies they invest in. Once that is achieved, I lay out an alternate plan whereby the system can transition to a private sector savings plan that would be far more lucrative than our present highly insecure Social Security system.

It is not my intention for this book to be a scholarly treatise on technology, economics, or politics. But I know how to think and like to think for myself. My career trained me to understand how systems work, to distinguish between cause and effect, and to "connect the dots" to be cognizant of the consequences of the modifications I propose to make on my system. So I question everything. Of course, I have my own prejudices, but they have evolved over time as I've acquired new information. I don't pretend to be a guru and my goal is not to win you over with all, or any, of my conclusions. Rather, my goal is to invite you to think for yourself and to keep the discussion alive and lively. The more discussion, the better. But remember to keep it respectful and not let it deteriorate into a rant.

I wish to stimulate discussion on these issues by showing where these experts, particularly those who influence policy, have gone wrong in the past and present. Let me know where I have influenced your thinking one way or another, particularly if you disagree with me and can enunciate those disagreements respectfully and courteously. Let's keep the dialogue going. I promise you that, regardless of whether you consider yourself Democrat, Republican, or neither, you will discover that we agree on far more than we disagree. As soon as we get past that hurdle, perhaps we will find a way to get things done right for a change.

We Have Gone Terribly Wrong

CHAPTER 1
POVERTY AMIDST PLENTY— WHY?

I am dismayed that we can no longer take for granted that the institutions we have relied upon all our lives are adequate to solve our current problems. I am equally perplexed because I see these institutions failing us at the very time our technology has reached the point of potentially providing abundance for the entire population of the world. We see this abundance everywhere, even in places that were written off a mere half-century ago as too far gone to be saved. But what has already been produced by technology has led to severe economic disruption, along with a call by our so-called "leaders" to rein in the abundance. They fear it and don't know how to handle it. Without discussing who benefits and who is hurt by deflation, they fear where it may lead. The institutions developed to handle scarcity do not operate well in an environment of such profusion.

Technology is the principal driver of abundance. That is obvious enough. But technology has also eliminated many jobs. Even back when I was a student, there was talk of the coming problem of industrial automation. Everyone seemed to understand that we were entering an advanced industrial era where the concept of "a day's work for a day's pay" no longer reigned supreme. Yet, none of the economic gurus of the time posited a solution. Without missing a beat, things remained in check, thanks to the power of the big unions and the monopoly power of the industrial juggernauts—General Motors, U.S. Steel, and Standard Oil. Nearly everyone who wanted to work could do so. They needed those jobs, too. Nobody wanted to live on welfare and bear the stigma attached to it. Besides, the wages in manufacturing provided a far better life than what welfare afforded. By today's standards, things were still a little rough around the edges, but they were good for most people.

In the latter part of the 20th century, starting around 1970, things started changing. Big business lost its hold on U.S. manufacturing for the U.S. market. Imports decimated domestic manufacturing and for much of the country's middle class, the '70s represented a turn for the worse in the face of the emerging global economy. What happened?

One of the most interesting aspects of my career in the oil industry was how it was, and is, intertwined with the global economy more than any other industry I can think of. As a young engineer working for Exxon in 1967 at its Fawley

Poverty Amidst Plenty — Why?

refinery in southern England, I watched as Israel prevailed over its Arab world adversaries in the Six Day War that June. This followed severe provocation from Egypt's Gamal Abdul Nasser and backed up by both Syria and Jordan.

What is not commonly known was that the Arabs blockaded oil to England and several other Western European nations because of their tacit support for the Israelis. The blockade failed because the U.S. still had surplus capacity and was able to make up England's shortfall. Before long, the refinery was processing Texas crude oil instead of the Libyan crude it was running before the embargo. Six short years later, following the Yom Kippur War, the U.S. was a net importer of oil and could no longer deflect the Arab boycott initiative. The price of oil rose precipitously and stayed there. Today, new extraction technologies are changing the landscape. The U.S. may soon become a net oil exporter once again. The price of oil has collapsed and perhaps will stay low for a long while. Our "experts" never expected this event, but fear that scenario, not knowing what to do with such abundance.

Though not connected, the U.S. dependence on foreign oil came not long after President Lyndon Johnson fought the Vietnam War and the War on Poverty without funding either one. And it was on the heels of President Nixon's opening to China. Neither chose to address the burgeoning burden of entitlement spending and no one inside or outside of their administrations understood that the global economy, then set in motion, would create an underclass of unemployables in this country. No president wants to raise taxes, decrease benefits, or discuss ugly truths on his watch. But the

Technology, Longevity, Economy, Liberty

deficiencies in addressing these issues have thrown the U.S. budget and balance of payments permanently out of balance. Promises were made then and continue to be made that simply cannot be kept without fiscal reform.

By the late '70s and early '80s, this arrangement, along with low priced imports, drove good jobs offshore in droves. Our industry was asleep and fell behind in both quality and price. The era of the "Rust Belt," characterized by outmoded shutdown factories and attendant unemployment, quickly evolved. The result was a steady reduction of the U.S. workforce as a percentage of the working age population. Our low-skilled jobs were shipped overseas. But the people with low work skills remained here and had to be provided for, one way or another.

At the same time, as if that weren't enough, advances in medical technology took a great leap forward. In one short generation, longevity has increased dramatically. I write this as I approach my 74th birthday. Although I may have slowed down a bit, I don't feel much different from how I felt when I reached 50. And I am not alone. My son Adam recently turned 50 and looks more like my father when he was 30 then when he was 50. In fact, at age 50 my father looked more like me at age 73!

This change has occurred with lightning speed. Because of technological advances, particularly since the advent of the computer age, information about how the human body functions has grown exponentially. This is good. People are living longer, healthier lives than ever before. Cures or treatments for life threatening illnesses have added years to

Poverty Amidst Plenty — Why?

the lives of innumerable people. Undoubtedly, however, that has burdened our economic system as even more non-working people must be provided for.

Therein is the triple whammy. Automation, the so-called "Global Economy," and longevity have permanently altered the social compact prevalent from at least the 1950s until the end of the 1960s. Since then, there has been a steady percentage decline in the workforce with more mouths to feed. Yes, technology has created abundance, even in parts of the world destined for disaster just a short while ago. These advances, particularly in our ability to acquire information, should have made us freer and more secure. We should be shouting praises for such technology, yet we're not. Our political and economic systems do not provide even a semblance of control. Our global economy feels like a house of cards ready to collapse at any moment, ushering in economic hardship and a loss of liberties as we have come to understand them.

So what is going on? One would assume that when the problems of scarcity are solved, humanity would enter a Golden Age. It's certainly achievable. But statistics indicate that one in six Americans still lives in poverty; not much fewer than in the '50s. There is a vast disparity between rich and poor. The technological golden goose has given rise to a new set of especially real problems. People who do not participate in the economy still fare badly, regardless of the underlying prosperity. Personal underachievement is on the rise as many just give up and rely on government largesse instead. But at what cost? Too many have lost the ability to participate meaningfully in the economy.

Technology, Longevity, Economy, Liberty

Despite their efforts, it seems that no one has come up with a workable solution to this dilemma. Yet we continue to be distracted by the many diversions around us. Welcome to the 21st century. The "Information Age" is upon us. But rather than discussing tough issues affecting us all, we are bombarded 24 hours a day with frivolous "information." While huge issues are staring us in the face, we opt to seek comfort from our Facebook "friends" who tell us what they've had for dinner, or where they had it, or what new trick their brilliant pooch just accomplished.

I don't mean to find fault when ordinary people find comfort in the ability to interact with a large group of people they cannot be in contact with personally. People derive great pleasure from such acts and far be it from me to deride such behavior. But I can't help feeling that the social media craze is just a manifestation of the ennui I referred to. Sharing one's activities with one's "friends" is, I suppose, a way of recognizing one's own accomplishments. I've heard that Facebook has become a problem for some as they read of the accomplishments, real or imaginary, of their friends and conclude that their own lives do not measure up. For them, Facebook merely exacerbates their poor sense of self.

Then there is the daily dose of information coming from sources we have always thought of as authoritative—the government, the New York Times, the BBC, Harvard, MIT. The pronouncements coming out of these once great institutions ring hollow to me and leave me with the feeling that they are simply hiding their uncertainty as they seek out

Poverty Amidst Plenty — Why?

answers themselves. Why else would there be such hostility to open discussion and alternate opinion?

There is a great disconnect in the economy; a vast mal-distribution of wealth. Amidst plenty, we still have a high poverty rate, caused by a) automation, b) little or no demand for low-skilled and unskilled labor, and c) the effect of longevity on the number of people living longer and longer past retirement. The result of the imbalance is a bloated, unsustainable federal budget, not only in the U.S., but everywhere.

The problem has loomed since the late '60s or early '70s and the only way the geniuses who run things figured out how to handle it was to run deficits and continue printing money. The problem has fed on itself. Republicans lowered taxes under Reagan and the second President Bush. The Democrats expanded welfare under Obama. Both parties ignored entitlement spending for Social Security and Medicare. Neither party admitted their solutions were a Band-Aid®. Now we are faced with a massive national debt that took 40 or so years to reach 50% of our annual GDP and a mere six years more for that debt to double. And how do our leaders respond? "No problem," they say. No debate. Case closed.

But wait a minute. Despite their efforts, they cannot close off debate. Because of today's Internet access, anyone can say anything. That is good. Arrogant authority needs to be questioned with its track record being far from reassuring. Zero interest rates have forced nearly everyone into a stock market more closely resembling a gambling casino than an investment vehicle. And this is a good thing? A vast underclass requiring permanent federal funding? This Band-Aid of a solution is not reassuring. And, Orwellian—bordering on dictatorial—efforts by these authorities to squelch debate are even worse.

Of course, the Internet can also be bad. Any crackpot can voice his opinions online. Few have the time or ability to check accuracy, so we are on our own. Is it any wonder why we are confused and frightened?

I started my adult life as a liberal Democrat, having come from a working class Jewish family. I am a first generation American and the first college-educated generation as well. I owe a lot, maybe everything, to free education. I had a superb high school education at Brooklyn Tech; as good as any I could have had at a top prep school at the time. At Cooper Union for the Advancement of Science and Art, I was fortunate enough to have received a free college education equal to what I could have received at MIT. I owe much to the public generosity that created Brooklyn Tech and the private generosity of Peter Cooper, a 19th century industrialist, who created Cooper Union. Being a liberal Democrat, to me, meant believing in private and public generosity in service of a better community.

Over the years, my views have not changed much, but my concept of what it means today to be a liberal Democrat certainly has. While I still believe in public generosity as well as private generosity, I also believe that the recipients should be obliged to demonstrate they deserve it and aren't automatically entitled. I believe they have a responsibility to do as much as they are capable of. That doesn't make me a right wing extremist. Even Karl Marx believed that. "From

Poverty Amidst Plenty — Why?

each according to his ability," he wrote. FDR believed it as well. His solution was to put the unemployed to work on conservation projects across the country. Even Bill Clinton agreed that our welfare system needed reform. And with the help of a Republican Congress, the job got done. None of the people on the left believed in sustaining a permanent underclass of unemployable individuals. Today, they would be derided by today's liberals for "blaming the victims."

I would argue that any government that promotes welfare programs that don't demand any responsibility from recipients acts as an enabler and immeasurably harms those recipients it purports to help. Could the leaders of such a government, one that creates dependency, perhaps have ulterior motives? I think they do. Once, in a cab in New Orleans driven by an island black in dreadlocks, I noticed a sign he posted: *When you've got them by the balls, their hearts and minds follow.* Initially startled by its insight and clarity, I soon realized what it says about human nature, master and slave. I have never forgotten that cab driver's cynical sign.

Could such leaders also create an environment where it is nearly impossible to hold a civil conversation with those professing opposing views? But, is it our views that really separate us, or is it our 'brand?' I recently became aware that people identify more with that than they do with the issue at hand. The Bipartisan Policy Center, released a study it performed that shed interesting light on that issue. Respondents were presented with two different education plans. Half were told that the first was a Democrat plan and the second was a Republican plan. The other half were told

Technology, Longevity, Economy, Liberty

the opposite. "[When] the specifics of Plan A were presented as the Democratic plan, Democrats preferred it by 75% to 17% and Republicans favored Plan B by 78% to 13%. When the exact same elements of A were presented in the exact same words, but as the Republican plan and with B as the Democrat plan, Democrats preferred B by 80% to 12%, while Republicans favored 'their party's plan' by 70% to 10% . . . In short, support for an identical plan shifted by more than 60 points among partisans, depending which party was said to back it."[2] That stunning result shows that party label is far more important than substance and demonstrates the herd mentality that has infected both parties.

The left and the right are equally guilty. Our institutions haven't kept pace with the technological advances that have led to mind blowing longevity increases and social awareness through an unfettered ability to obtain information. The fact that the information can be true, false, or indifferent is a tremendous problem that causes me stress and sleepless nights. Our authoritative sources sound way off the mark to me for good reason. They are. Maybe the tried and true, which, incidentally, only worked so-so 50 or 100 years ago, is hopelessly irrelevant today. So, how does the average Joe cope?

I am not a fan of nostalgia. Technology has raised the mass of humanity out of the rough, short life it endured before the industrial revolution. My patience runs thin for those who condemn our technological advances, or those who tell us that we have to change our ways to avoid technologically-induced environmental catastrophe. Catastrophe? What catastrophe? I recall a great cartoon in the New Yorker a while back. Three

Poverty Amidst Plenty — Why?

or four cavemen were sitting around a fire. The one talking is discussing their fate. "Our water is pure. Our air is also pure. Our meat is all free range. So why are we dying at age 35?"

Why indeed! The answer should be obvious. Because human ingenuity, geared to improving life for humanity, has succeeded wildly. Yes, there are downsides. We should be aware of them and deal with them. We have. I have spent a large chunk of my career addressing the downsides. The pollutants in our air and water are a tiny fraction of what they were when I entered industry in 1964. I am the first to admit that there are huge imperfections in the tools of my trade. But we are tasked with finding ways to improve the lives of the many, not just the privileged few and we do the best we can. That means driving costs down, sometimes at the expense of a pristine environment. We strike that balance and we make mistakes sometimes. We are only human and we do not deserve the venom so frequently heaped upon us by many. I get defensive when technology is judged negatively without acknowledgment of the good it has done.

There are even extremists among them who actually see humanity itself as the problem and wish it ill. I think they have too much power and influence over the tone of the discussion in ways that distort public perception. For example, I recently saw a bumper sticker on a very ordinary Toyota RAV4, "*GOP—Gas Oil Pigs.*" What could possibly cause someone to condemn so vehemently the very commodities he owes his entire standard of living to? I say it is the work of extremists who refuse to admit that there is a powerful upside to technology and advance occurs at its pace. I think most people who care about the environment, and I am one of them, have the welfare of humanity at heart. But too many in the forefront have created such a false negative picture with sensational pronouncements that resonate with the public. Some look at the modern world and are disgusted at what it has done to nature. They see their role as arresting this development, often at great disadvantage for the people affected. William McKibben is such an advocate. He wrote an influential book called *The End of Nature*. Consider David M. Graber's Los Angeles Times' review of that book:

> "McKibben," Graber says, "is a bio-centrist, and so am I. We are not interested in the utility of a particular species or free-flowing river, or ecosystem to mankind. They have intrinsic value, more value—to me—than another human body, or a billion of them. Human happiness, and certainly human fecundity, are not as important as a wild and healthy planet. I know social scientists who remind me that people are part of nature, but it isn't true. Somewhere along the line—at about a billion (sic) years ago, maybe half that—we quit the contract and became a cancer. We became a plague upon ourselves and upon the Earth. It is cosmically unlikely that the developed world will choose to end its orgy of fossil energy consumption, and the Third World its suicidal consumption of landscape. Until such time as *Homo Sapiens* should decide to rejoin nature, some of us can only hope that the right virus will come along." [3]

Poverty Amidst Plenty — Why?

I realize that most of our so-called "experts" do not wish humanity ill. But, I have trouble with them using fancy words and unproven concepts that obscure the fundamental problems and provide bogeymen to deflect the unease felt by many.

Take the issue of the widening gap between the rich and poor. It doesn't take formal training to understand the cause of this trend. Even during the '50s, the so-called Golden Age of Prosperity, many people worried, rightfully so, about the impact of automation on the economy. What would happen when jobs done by people were phased out and replaced by machines? At the time, it was an academic question which was largely ignored. As it turned out, however, that was not the only question affecting the future of the economy. There were less obvious ones. What happens when people live 20 or 30 years after they retire without contributing to the economy? They'd still need goods and services. What happens in a global economy when even the few jobs left can be done by capable workers at far lower wages than the inflated wages of American workers negotiated before the economy went global? It seems to me that these are the fundamental problems we face that are being neglected. These problems, if not resolved, will do us in as a nation much sooner than any of our environmental problems, which we have been steadily solving without much fanfare for almost as long as I have been active in industry.

CHAPTER 2
INDUSTRIAL TECHNOLOGY AND ITS CRITICS

The industrial revolution transformed humanity with the invention of machines, devices that convert the heat of combustion into motion and produce work. Machines performed tasks previously accomplished by animals, beasts of burden, or humans—slaves, serfs, or servants. The development of the steam engine was an early manifestation of the industrial revolution. Energy released by the burning of coal produces steam from water in a confined chamber. As the steam expands, pressure increases until it overwhelms the force holding it back (usually a valve in the system). Then the steam releases its pressure against a turbine or wheel, causing it to revolve. This movement can be harnessed to provide work or transportation.

The steam engine was the first of many inventions that harvested the energy created by a burning source into work, the ability to overcome a force, or into motion, another form of work. Engines became available to safely transport goods and men at great speeds, giving rise to the railroads.

The steam engine also gave rise to canal construction to transport newly invented steam boats as a means of moving goods from point of production to point of consumption. Moving goods by steam engines over land or water made specialization possible, giving rise to factories where goods could be mass produced and shipped to where they would be purchased and consumed. Ease of transportation was the key. And in those newly minted factories, coal was used as a fuel to run other machines in the manufacturing process as the art of utilizing the energy from the burning of coal became more refined and widespread.

Refrigeration created the next great breakthrough. Physical chemists discovered that by manipulating the physical conditions of certain compounds, cold temperatures could be produced from machines powered by fuels—the exact same source as transportation and work. Every compound has a specific boiling point that increases with internal pressure. For example, a compound with a normal boiling point (boiling point without imposing any additional pressure) of minus eight degrees, can be compressed in a machine to a pressure where its boiling point is 100 degrees. Then it can be condensed with air or water as a coolant at that pressure. When the pressure is then released to normal pressure, it will flash and reach its normal boiling point of minus eight degrees.

Industrial Technology and its Critics

We now have a substance capable of cooling things down—a refrigerant. Counterintuitively to the layman, harnessing combustion also created the ability to produce refrigeration and keep things cold.

Originally used to make ice commercially, refrigeration allowed long distance hauling of perishable foods—fish, meat, fruit, and vegetables. As the technology became more developed, ice boxes were introduced into houses, followed by refrigerators. Further along, the development of air conditioning made it inviting to comfortably live in places with tropical conditions. As I said, refrigeration made it possible to haul perishables long distances. It also made it possible to store them at home, adding to the abundance brought about by technological advancements. Air conditioning did as much . . . and even more.

The power of machines was measured in "horsepower." A steam engine could produce the same amount of transportation as just as many horses, but exceeded what they could do. Three hundred horses, for example, could not duplicate the accomplishment of a 300 horsepower engine. Machines deriving their power from combustion afforded inventors and engineers the chance to dream big, to conquer the skies, or the tropics, and make life more than drudgery for much of humanity. Until recent years, however, the benefits of technology were only available in the developed world. Now, they are reaching many places considered by many to be hopelessly impoverished only a few years ago.

There were great downsides to the use of combustion energy, particularly from coal lacking pollution abatement

Technology, Longevity, Economy, Liberty

technology. I am fascinated by much of the art of the early period of industrialization, which revealed previously strictly rural scenes with factory smokestacks belching black smoke into the air. In the country, this was a minimal nuisance. But in the cities, the pollution was awful. Even there, though, the pollution was tolerated, because the upside was tremendous. Lives were enriched, which is amazing if you think about, say, the novels of Charles Dickens depicting the lives of street urchins during the days of the industrial revolution. Life in those times does not appeal to me. So, if industrial pollution was tolerated back then, I can only imagine what life was like for the dispossessed underclass before the benefits of industrialization.

Even my experience, living in the Brooklyn slums a century later, did not seem much better. My boyhood Brooklyn was still largely powered by coal, dirty coal. Some say that all coal is dirty. True enough, but then, as late as the 1950s, houses were heated with coal and electricity came from coal burning power plants with little or no pollution abatement equipment. In Pittsburgh, where I have spent much of my adult life, I hear even worse stories about life in this industrial city before the advent of pollution control.

So, I find it interesting, amazing even, that despite the clearly evident downside, industrialization was accepted. Why? Because industrialization made the once unavailable great power of machines available. Industrialization led to emancipation of the serfs in Europe and probably would have led to the freeing of slaves in the U.S. had not the Civil War already settled the issue.

Industrial Technology and its Critics

It took us a century or more to deal with the problems of labor exploitation initially, and later with industrial pollution, and we've made quite a bit of progress since then. For the present, I want to concentrate on the positive aspects of industrialization and the efforts to ameliorate the pollution problems. Of course, issues associated with the labor component of the mix also need to be addressed.

It wasn't until the 1960s that our wealth as a country made us question why we tolerated air and water pollution to the extent we had. Certainly, others talked and wrote about it prior to that. But the environmental movement did not take off until then. As newlyweds in 1963, my wife and I took a motor trip across the country. We became aware of the smog in Los Angeles while stuck in freeway traffic. The radio weather reports included the degree of eye irritation expected each day. But LA smog did not prevent people from moving there, which says a lot.

Nevertheless, President Nixon initiated the EPA (Environmental Protection Agency) in 1970. That's right– Nixon. I was with Exxon at the time and had worked on a couple of studies to determine the cost of fixes designed to improve air and water quality. These studies formed part of the industry's negotiations with the EPA that determined the course of regulation as there was no point in promulgating rules that were too costly or could not be met in a timely manner. At the time, the EPA tried to be an honest broker and accepted that the public at large ultimately pays the price for environmental improvement. The EPA, even more than

Technology, Longevity, Economy, Liberty

industry, strived to make sure that the improvement was worth the price. I wish I could say that was still the case.

The first wave of regulation tackled more obvious issues, such as particulate emission from smoke stacks—the once familiar black plumes—and acid rain, the result of sulfur dioxide reacting with rainwater and producing small quantities of sulfuric acid. Fixes were known but expensive. They had to be done in stages to keep prices in check. Sometimes the public was impatient with the progress. Sometimes their impatience was justified. Sometimes anti-industry zealots fed the impatience by spreading untruths. But the job got done. Within a few years, all those black plumes disappeared from the landscape, as did the preponderance of acid rain.

It is important to note how long it took for these environmental regulations to promulgate. By the 1960s, the country was already extremely wealthy by most objective standards. We had left the communist world in the dust. The contrast in Europe between western democracies and those dominated by the Soviet Union were astonishing. This was most obvious in Berlin where western democracy and free enterprise stood in stark contrast to Soviet dictatorship and socialism. The contrast was so great, in fact, that the Soviets had to build the Berlin Wall to keep the East Berliners in. President Kennedy delivered his famous "Ich bin ein Berliner" speech, inviting the world to visit Berlin if they thought communism was the wave of the future. And true to form, pollution abatement lagged far behind in the communist world. Those economies barely had sufficient capacity to clothe, feed, and

Industrial Technology and its Critics

shelter their inhabitants. Clean air and water was a luxury they simply could not afford.

This is a point I wish to emphasize. Pollution control is only acceptable by the affected population after the basic needs of its people are satisfied. It was true then, it is true today, and it will be true tomorrow. That is why pollution, the downside of industrialization, was, and still is, tolerated until society becomes affluent enough to afford to deal with it. Because the positives so greatly outweigh the negatives, the black air it spawns is preferable to missing out on the industrial technology.

That is my fundamental problem with trying to apply our concept of environmentalism universally. We in the west have come to a point in time where we can afford pollution abatement without much of an economic downside. But foisting our ideas on the developing world puts a burden on them that has significant negative effects—even deadly ones.

Rachel Carson wrote *Silent Spring* in 1962 and received the Presidential Medal of Freedom by Jimmy Carter. She is considered an icon today. But as a result of her writing, the chemical pesticide DDT was banned in the United States and, subsequently, in the entire world. I do not wish to disparage Carson's thesis about the harmful effects of DDT. I merely note that her warnings came only after malaria was wiped out in the developed world. Such banning could not have affected her longevity or health personally. But the subsequent premature banning or limited use of DDT in the third world likely caused too many there to die needlessly, thereby causing more harm than good to affected populations. So, if I see such overreach

Technology, Longevity, Economy, Liberty

on the part of environmentalists, making pronouncements from which they are personally exempt, as harmful elitism, I believe I am on solid ground.

In case you haven't noticed, this is an age of plenty. Many people are living lives today which would have been called luxurious just a couple generations ago. Back then, it was rare for middle class families to have two cars, air conditioning, dishwashers, or any number of items considered basic today. Only the luxury cars had exclusive features that are now standard on even the lowest ticket cars of this era. Today, people who are classified as living in poverty generally have items not even available one or two short decades ago—flat screen color TVs and smartphones, just to name the obvious.

Yet there are those who continue to forecast gloom and doom. This is far from a new phenomenon. In 1968, Professor Paul Ehrlich made several startling predictions in *The Population Bomb*, declaring it was too late to prevent mass starvation in India. He also asserted it was too late to prevent England from disappearing because of the problems with pollution.

The New York Times recently carried a story called "The Unrealized Disaster of Population Explosion."[4] Prof. Ehrlich, the authors stated, remains unrepentant. In fact, he says if he had written the book today, he would be even more apocalyptic. In addition to mass starvation, others predicted both nuclear and environmental disaster in the developed world. Of course, nothing of the kind has occurred. England still stands. India is flourishing. China may soon have the world's highest Gross Domestic Product. How can so many "authorities" like Professor Ehrlich have reached so many wrong conclusions? And, an even more vexing question: Why do we still persist in listening to them?

Over the past couple of generations, more people have emerged from poverty to middle class life than in the entire prior history of human civilization. Such progress is being jeopardized today by similar cries of authorities that we are on the path to disaster. This recent progress was not miraculous, but rather was the direct result of the benefits gained by industrial production. Costs of production have plummeted as the developed world passed on technology to less developed countries. Now we have oil refineries, steel mills, and other basic industries all over the world. All this basic industry has been overbuilt. That deserves to be repeated: BASIC INDUSTRY HAS BEEN OVERBUILT.

We now have an overcapacity problem. Note: The word "problem" should be in quotation marks. Why? Because most people would recognize that scarcity is a problem, but few would comprehend that a glut can be just as problematic. Again, why? Overcapacity is another word for low demand and low demand leads to shuttering excess capacity which creates unemployment. And unemployment leads to government intervention in the form of a) unemployment insurance payments and b) all manner of welfare payments. This has led to bloated budgets and, recently, to trillion dollar deficits.

My take away from that turn of events is that economists really have no solid ideas on how to handle that abundance. As I said, I live in Pittsburgh. We experienced the "great recession" of 2008–9 just like everywhere else. Yet, if you did not read the newspapers or other accounts, the evidence of it hitting the vast majority was not apparent. Restaurants were full. Sporting and music events attracted many patrons. There were no bread lines. It was certainly an improvement over the situation during the Great Depression of the '30s. I suspect that, even then, the problem was not scarcity. Rather, it was a fluke in the way economics works and the inability of the authoritative economists to develop better ways of handling the normal cyclical fluctuation, though at times severe, that accompanies any system.

Throughout the long history of mankind, scarcity was the principal driver of upheaval that motivated people to war and conquest. Humans were forced into competition to survive, to be the recipient of the earth's limited bounty. The Industrial Revolution slowly changed that dynamic. Scarcity is no longer the principal driver of conflict or poverty. Technology has provided the wherewithal to create surplus and wealth for all of the earth's human population. Our other institutions—politics and economics—have not kept up.

Even worse than that inability are those authorities who imply, wrongly so in my opinion, that such a state of abundance is unsustainable. Sustainability is the new buzzword. We are ruining life for future generations, they say.

When I entered the workforce in 1964 with a freshly minted master's degree and a coveted job in big oil, nobody ever suspected it would be possible to provide sufficient energy to virtually eliminate poverty in the world. None of us, even those at the vanguard, suspected that such abundance would be universally available today. Billions of people around the world, we thought, would be condemned to short, rough lives and many would starve for lack of adequate nourishment. Pulling many billions out of poverty with a still steady rise in the world's population is an accomplishment that was unthinkable when I began my career.

It is easy to understand how affluent people can condemn the downside of technology. If I am comfortably warm in my 3,000 square foot house in suburban Pittsburgh, with my late model Buick sedan and Toyota 4Runner SUV in the garage, drinking cold water from a plastic bottle and munching on fruits grown in California as I sit in front of my 86" flat screen TV, manufactured in China and shipped on vessels powered by marine diesel refined in Texas from oil produced in Saudi Arabia, I would, nevertheless, be upset if I had to look out my window and observe a black plume of smoke belching out of a nearby factory chimney or smell the acrid aroma. Perhaps I would be just as upset if, instead of seeing that scene as I looked out my window, I saw it on my giant screen in a place like Ethiopia. Perhaps I would feel righteous and believe that we need to do something to spare those poor Ethiopians from such pollution. However, Ethiopians might have a different opinion and insist they should not be spared such pollution if it involves their being deprived of the energy required to grow their economy. "If the deal is to abandon the upside of industrialization, don't even think of depriving me of that in favor of your conception of what is good for me," is the expected response. Likewise, people in the emerging nations, such as India and China, want no part of such deprivation. I think they're right.

Most opponents of industrialization are sincere and have the long term welfare of humanity in mind when they wish a curtailment of industrialization. Yet, there is the NIMBY phenomenon— "Not in my backyard!" No one wants to live near a factory, a steel mill, an oil refinery, or a slaughterhouse. Who can blame them?

This animosity becomes overblown when there is some kind of disaster. The BP Deepwater Horizon oil blowout is a good example. Every day, scary images of a high pressure out-of-control blowout filled the air waves. It appeared that the U.S. Gulf Coast was about to be destroyed. Every day an oil-soaked bird was shown on TV being attended to by a naturalist. To my skeptical eye, though, it seemed as if it was the same bird being shown each time.

I have my own theories about the event and its coverage. For one thing, I believe that the actual amount of oil spilled into the Gulf was a fraction of the estimated 60,000 barrels per day. I believe that a greater volume of gas, rather than oil, was released—gas that was quickly dissipated. In my opinion, what was observed on TV was the displacement of sea water by the gas, because it is gas, not oil that creates the high pressure in oil formations. Gas creates the gushers, not oil. Pressurized oil in the absence of much gas would have quickly dissipated. Why did BP not defend itself with such an explanation? I am not sure, but I suspect it would have been accused of covering up. Oil companies are easy targets and their CEOs are loath to exacerbate relations even further. They just take it, knowing full well that, though the world might hate oil companies, it could not get along for very long without their products.

Industrial Technology and its Critics

Regardless of whether or not my theory is correct, life has returned to normal all along the Gulf Coast with no long lasting damage. Gulf front real estate is as desirable and expensive as ever. Fishing has resumed and life is good. Nevertheless, fueled by inherent hatred of oil companies and the constant drumbeat of climate change, there is the clamor of well-meaning people urging the end of oil exploration in the U.S. Gulf and elsewhere. They are misinformed.

I ask these well-intentioned people, "How much of your lifestyle are you willing to give up to further the end you are demanding?" Too many people, urged on by much of the media, are unable or unwilling to connect the dots. Oil exploration is necessary to replace the 80 million barrels consumed each day to make products we all need and use—gasoline, diesel fuel, all manner of plastics and petrochemicals, and even our pharmaceuticals—and run our technological world.

Is it so bad that millions of people who were written off as beyond saving a mere generation ago have access to these life-affirming goods? In China alone, the demand for petroleum-based products has been increasing by an additional one million barrels per day each year. I am sure that just about every Chinese individual whose life has been enhanced by access to these products still accepts the terrible pollution in the cities in China. And, you can be sure that in the near future as prosperity hits the tipping point, there will be a clamor to improve environmental conditions.

By then, prosperity will have spread to the regions of the planet that remain dirt poor: Africa, many Arab countries, and

South America. Industrial technology is here to stay because it is a boon to humans. As long as people clamor to improve their lives, there will be sufficient incentive to keep on developing.

Should we be cognizant of the damage we do to the environment? Certainly. Will we run out of oil eventually? Maybe. A wise man once remarked that the Stone Age did not end because we ran out of stones. We simply found a better way to live that did not involve fashioning our implements from stone. Similarly with petroleum. There will come a day, not too far in the future, that deriving our energy needs by burning fossil fuels will be supplanted by something more economic and cleaner. My hunch is that it will be some form of terrestrial energy based on nuclear fusion or fission. And, it is my belief, that when that day comes, the cost of energy will be far lower than it is today and will be cleaner as well.

Industrial Technology and its Critics

CHAPTER 3
INFORMATION TECHNOLOGY AND AUTOMATION

My dad was a cornball. I often laughed at his ironic jokes anyway. I recall this particular one.

"Ancient Babylonia was very advanced," he started.

I took the bait. "How so?"

"When they dug it up, they found no wires."

"Okay, I give up. How does that prove they were advanced?"

He answered with his inimitable grin. "It shows they had wireless there."

Dad was no fool. He understood wireless. Of course, the wireless my dad knew was a mere fraction of the behemoth it has become. For Dad, wireless meant radio and later TV. Now it means connecting instantaneously with anyone, anywhere with minimal effort and with nearly all the information ever

Technology, Longevity, Economy, Liberty

accumulated. And the experts tell us, after 100 years, it is still in its infancy.

The world has changed much in the 50 plus years since I received my BS degree in Chemical Engineering. Even as little as 25 years ago, with the search engines at our disposal and the power of personal computers then, I never would have imagined how much we could have progressed in such a short time.

And computational speed is now almost a sideshow in the information age compared with data access; I can compare engineering methods in the '60s with present day. In 1964, I joined Esso Research and Engineering Company (now Exxon). We had access to one IBM 360 computer, which occupied almost an entire room. A staff of computer technicians ran the beast and data entry was by punch card. Each piece of data needed to be entered on a separate card and computer specialists were trained to develop programs in FORTRAN, a computer language now part of the distant past.

We all used the same machine and, because of the cost of computing, time was rationed among departments. Accounting needed the bulk of the time available, despite the obvious need we engineers had to perform calculations for the chemical and refinery plants we were designing. Even so, Esso was way more advanced than most of the other companies performing similar calculations. We had great programs written in FORTRAN with super acronyms, such as ASPECT (**A**dvanced **S**tage-by-stage **P**rogram for **E**ngineering **C**omplex **T**owers) and COPE (**CO**mputerized **P**rocess **E**ngineering).

Information Technology and Automation

The people who wrote these programs were geniuses. We mere mortals only used them.

Even with these computer tools, progress was not much faster—maybe even slower—than the shortcut methods engineers used prior to their availability. What they did, however, was save significant cost as they allowed us to design with smaller margin of error. But, because of the scant running time available to us, we had only one shot per day at a solution. And we were charged for the computer time. Engineers who made frequent computer errors caused "bomb outs" without a solution and were easily identified. Engineers who habitually took too much time to reach an optimal solution did not last long.

Today, the average laptop or desktop computer packs much more wallop than that old IBM 360. Recently, I had occasion to consult on a project for the company I retired from a few years earlier. The young engineer simulated the plant on his laptop using a computer program similar to ASPECT and COPE combined—the simulation tools I used at Esso. But what a difference! The young engineer projected the result on a screen in our conference room. We asked numerous "what if" questions and received nearly immediate answers. In one afternoon, we accomplished what would have taken a month in 1964 and was not even possible a few years before that. At that rate, we have completed our studies for developing the best solution for the company to produce "ultra-ultra" low sulfur gasoline needed for the super energy efficient engines of the future, no doubt being developed using similar tools at auto company design centers

Technology, Longevity, Economy, Liberty

in Detroit, Germany, Japan, and Korea. In the near future, many other emerging countries will have similar technical expertise. Information technology is helping to keep the cost down for improving industrial products while also improving the environment.

But, as I previously alluded to, that same information technology is contributing to massive unemployment by replacing humans with machines. When I received my education in the '60s, the problem was already looming. Now computers and robots are commonplace.

I did consulting work briefly at an electro-galvanizing plant owned jointly by a major steel and auto company. The plant used electric current to dissolve zinc electrodes into a bath so it could be plated out on a rolling sheet of steel that passed through the bath. The galvanizing process, now common, keeps the steel used for autos from rusting out quickly. Now, cars on the road, even in the rough northern environments, no longer rust out in four or five years.

Robots controlled the electro-galvanizing process, measured the electric current applied and automatically replaced the zinc electrodes just before they were totally dissolved into the solution. The entire process was fascinating to observe and operated with practically zero labor. I had the advanced skills needed to ensure that the process worked as efficiently as possible. But, less skilled or unskilled labor was no longer needed, as robots performed the jobs.

Millions of such jobs have already disappeared and similar losses are on the horizon. Case in point—consider ordering a sandwich at your local convenience store. Instead of a human,

Information Technology and Automation

a machine takes your order. It even personalizes it. White, wheat, or rye? Rye. No problem. Mustard or mayo? Mustard. Fine.

Now there is a push to increase the minimum wage to as high as $15 per hour as if high wages were not already sending massive amounts of low-skilled jobs overseas and converting even more jobs to tasks done by machines. The problem of employment for low-skilled people will only get worse. Politicians ostensibly working to better the lives of low-skilled workers surely understand this. But they persist in using rhetoric that places the blame on greed and not where it belongs—on automation and the global economy. By doing so, they harm the very constituencies they purport to help. That obfuscation may sell, but at what cost?

Before long, even technical jobs requiring formal post high school education will disappear. Knowledge is power and knowledge—information technology, in particular—is getting more and more concentrated, rivaling inherited wealth as the source of vast income inequality. Move over Carnegie and Vanderbilt and Rockefeller. Make way for the folks who own and/or create information products used in everything we do.

Yes. Make way for those who own their intellectual property. Isn't that the key to success? They have choices. If they are unhappy with high wage scales in the U.S., they set up factories in China or India. Information age heroes, such as Gates, Jobs, and others, have done just that. Even people who do not need factories of their own can contract with a Chinese manufacturer to make components for their products. The Chinese certainly beat U.S. labor rates prices nearly every time. They rig the game by keeping their currency undervalued.

The result? Owners of intellectual property become rich while providing cheap products to consumers. But the low-skilled are left out of the picture. No wonder there is a vast and growing disparity between the rich and poor in this country. This is quite obvious and not at all complicated. It has little or nothing to do with class warfare or any of the epithets thrown at it by politicians with an agenda or by economists who cling to old concepts of wealth and poverty. No, the days of the Robber Barons are over and trying to cure present day poverty with the tool and rhetoric of the early 20th century is a fool's, or charlatan's, errand.

Information Technology and Automation

CHAPTER 4
TECHNOLOGY AND LONGEVITY

The advances in longevity are perhaps the most amazing technological accomplishments of all. Social Security legislation dates to the thirties. As young adults, my parents were raising their family then. The Social Security Act was meant to provide some protection for the few indigent seniors who lived past the retirement age of 65. A scant percentage of the population lived much longer than that milestone. Fatal diseases, like tuberculosis and polio, once incurable, are now nearly obsolete. Cancer used to be a death sentence, as was, in many cases, tuberculosis. Phil Zimmerman, a teenage friend of my brother Lenny, contracted Hodgkin's disease as a teenager and died within a year. My cousin, Arnold Miller, died of cancer as a young man, shortly after his wedding.

Technology, Longevity, Economy, Liberty

My immediate family provides interesting anecdotal insight, and I am sure that many families have had similar histories. My mother died in 1947 at the age of 38, after suffering from cancer for several years. I believe it was stomach cancer, but I can't be certain, as record keeping was not as precise back then. Perhaps the cancer started somewhere else and metastasized to a vital organ. At that time, cancer usually was found too late and there were no treatments, such as chemotherapy or radiation that had much effect.

In that same year, my last remaining grandparents, Tobias, my father's father, and Hannah, my mother's mother, died as well. They were both in their 60s.

Two of the three of my father's siblings succumbed to heart attacks in their 50s. My father almost died of a sudden heart attack at 57 in 1966, but was saved by an expert medical team. He came out of it with congestive heart failure and managed to make it another seven years, until just before his 64th birthday in 1973.

The next generation of those three siblings consists of four men and three women. I am the youngest, at 74 as of this writing. My brother and sister are 83 and 78, respectively. My uncle Raphael's two sons are both in their 80s and my aunt Ruth's two daughters are in their late 70s. All seven of us are healthy. Actuarially, our life expectancies are in the late 80s or early 90s, possibly longer.

Dad and his siblings all smoked. My siblings and I are on statin medications. I am less certain about my cousins, but suspect they are on similar regimens, which are common and effective. All of us have slowed a bit, but are still full of vitality.

Technology and Longevity

None of us look much older than our parents looked when they were in their 50s.

Much of the medical progress that has occurred over the last few decades is the result of hi-tech computing—the ability to crunch the massive amounts of data needed to develop the statistical information on causes and potential cures for all sorts of diseases. Industrial technology has permitted us to do things previously impossible without high powered machinery, like flying. Likewise, information technology has permitted us to do formerly implausible things. This data crunching is the very reason they've come so far so fast.

So, a combination of healthier lifestyles, effective drugs, and better diagnostic information and procedures has changed the equation. Much more is to come. I recently read a headline on the cover of *Time* magazine that predicted a lifespan of 140 in the near future, maybe even in the next generation. The prediction is that the first person to reach 150 years of age has already been born. [5] If that comes to pass, even if, optimistically, the number of new births levels out at two per couple, five generations will coexist and the world's population would grow to about 12 billion, a 70% increase above today's and more than three times the population when Dr Ehrlich made his apocalyptic predictions in *The Population Bomb*. What is more, the working population will be no larger than it is today. That is truly frightening and will take far more human ingenuity to deal with this than we have required so far.

If we do not want an even greater overhang of unnecessarily poor, badly serviced population, we need to realize that we are truly in uncharted territory. New methods

Technology, Longevity, Economy, Liberty

will be needed in the political and economic sectors or there will be huge problems. I cannot be certain—nothing is—but I expect technology will be capable of handling the population's needs with a semblance of abundance. I foresee the end of the age of fossil fuels in favor of nuclear energy.

The unsung side benefit of increased carbon dioxide in the atmosphere has been a correspondingly large increase in the yields of crops. Perhaps that is the key to why, even with the world's population twice as high as when Dr. Ehrlich made his dire predictions, we have been able to stave off human starvation. So, unlike most, I worry about the end of the fossil fuel age more than I worry about global warming.

The longevity explosion will lead to a new set of problems as four, or even five, generations have to coexist. That, perhaps, even more than automation or the global economy, will force a new look at solving poverty problems caused by this new world order.

Technology and Longevity

CHAPTER 5
WAR AND TECHNOLOGY

The frightening and actual downside of technology is mechanized conflict, particularly nuclear. In previous chapters, I wrote glowing reviews of technology's benefits. But mechanized warfare has created unsurpassed catastrophe. By the time of the Civil War, ironclad construction already had replaced wood as the preferred substance for naval vessels. "Steam propulsion had begun to be applied to warships." [6] Naval warfare would never be the same again. The battle of the Monitor and the Merrimack caused worldwide attention and set the stage for the use of 20th century battleships, aircraft carriers, and submarines using even more advanced technologies. The Civil War claimed a million lives—a shocking number far greater than the number killed in prior wars in the U.S.

Technology, Longevity, Economy, Liberty

The age of flight had an even more devastating impact on warfare by permitting bombardment from the air. The devastation only affected the combatants during World War I, but by World War II, as carpet bombing became perfected, extraordinary numbers of civilians suffered. It may be partly true that warfare has created the most prolific use of technology. There is a sick joke that made the rounds among us engineers. "How do mechanical engineers and civil engineers differ? Mechanical engineers build weapons; civil engineers build targets."

The development of the atom bomb had a sobering effect on the world— on the people who developed it (mostly socially conscious scientists), on the people who used it, on President Truman, the military, the people of the United States, Japan (the victimized country), and, in fact, the entire world. We've lived in fear of nuclear war since then, knowing that would almost certainly end human life on earth.

The human toll from mechanized warfare, including mechanized genocide, that occurred in the industrial era, late 19th century onward, certainly exceeded all deaths from prior warfare. Yet warfare persists. I fault our institutions for their failure to reduce the threat of war. Perhaps when scarcity was the norm, competition for the necessities of life made war an inevitable aspect of the human condition. Wasn't "lebensraum" the Nazi German justification for its expansionism? Wasn't their excuse for exterminating the Jews that they, the Jews, were responsible for their defeat and their loss of territory? Scarcity, whether actual or fabricated—scarcity of land, resources, food, the necessities of life—has always been used to justify warfare.

War and Technology

Today, more than any other time in history, war cannot be justified by that rationalization because we have the capacity for abundance, even as much of the world still suffers from scarcity. It is not technology that causes this to remain the case, but it will be technology that will cause unheard of suffering, possibly even the end of humanity should a third world war, complete with nuclear weapons in the hands of so many nations, break out. That thought keeps me awake at night. Our political and economic institutions have not caught up with technological innovation. The impact created horror in the 20th century. Technology became the servant of the worst elements of human existence and power. Under the dictatorial policies of fascists and communists, the world suffered perhaps a hundred million deaths in useless war after useless war. The technology to inflict mass destruction must be kept out of the hands of tyrants. That job, unfortunately, fell upon the United States and I see no other power that can, or will, pick up the mantle should we abandon it.

In the aftermath of World War II, the United States assumed the mantle of Superpower. With it came the responsibility to police the world's conflicts. Ordinary Americans have paid a dear price for this and, naturally, do not like it. I would prefer to call American power "Pax Americana," American-led peace. But there has been little peace. First came the Berlin airlift that saved West Berlin from Soviet domination, then there was Korea, a war that ended without a clear victor. It is a war we are still fighting with nukes now in the hands of the North Koreans. We inherited the mess in

Technology, Longevity, Economy, Liberty

Indochina from the French which led to our involvement in Vietnam. But even the "victorious" Vietnamese still look to the U.S. for protection from Chinese interference.

I may not like it, but I see no alternative to American power as an antidote to the bad guys. Many call me a warmonger for that position, but for similar reasons, others called Churchill a warmonger as well, until it was too late to stop the unspeakable carnage of World War II. Nobody offered Mr. Churchill the Nobel Peace Prize. But seeking peace through strength and deterrence is a far nobler goal than seeking a Nobel Prize for peace by looking the other way and avoiding a conflict until it is way too late. Too many Peace Prizes were awarded to such individuals.

Technology opened the door for ushering in a long lasting golden era for humanity. It has also created the possibility of annihilation through nuclear disaster. There are huge imperfections in the tools of my trade—engineering. We solve one problem only to create another; then solve that one and create another, and on and on it goes. But, by and large, I believe in technology and believe it can ultimately bring about the sustainable solution we should be seeking. But, as I said, it can also create calamity. It is not clear whether we will blow ourselves up or create a world in which the lion can indeed lie down with the lamb.

Perhaps, more than any other reason, the fear of unnecessary war, particularly nuclear conflagration, has made me wish to examine our institutions to see what could and should be done differently to make ordinary people more secure and, therefore, less likely to follow tyrants or to demand violent solutions or revolutions to solve their very real problems.

CHAPTER 6
ECONOMIC REALITIES

What has been the principal source of our economic problems? A case can be made that it stems from our status as a Superpower. In 1953, immediately after Dwight Eisenhower became president, he took action to end the Korean conflict in order to negotiate a division with the communist-ruled north and, in alliance with the U.S., the democratically-ruled south. The Supreme Commander, who led the charge to defeat Hitler, hated war and realized its real cost in blood and treasure. The armistice he engineered, however, has not been without problems and, in some ways, the conflict still persists. Later on in his presidency, Ike inherited the Vietnam mess after the French were defeated at Dien Bien Phu. He negotiated a similar agreement with the Ho Chi Minh to respect the division of Vietnam. Later on, he acted quickly to quell the Anglo, French, and Israeli invasion of Egypt after Nasser unilaterally nationalized the Suez Canal. In each of these incidents, he moved to minimize the extent of armed hostility that he knew could invoke a third world conflict.

Things changed rapidly after Ike left office. President Kennedy certainly outdid Ike in charisma, but was no match for him when it came to understanding the debilitating impact of warfare. As a result, shortly after his election, JFK was easy prey. He was convinced to put together a force of Cuban exiles to invade and retake Cuba from Castro. Eisenhower never would have authorized such foolishness. The Bay of Pigs fiasco was an embarrassment, but it did not chasten Kennedy; it simply emboldened Moscow. Shortly after that, we had the Cuban Missile Crisis—a crisis that nearly ended in disaster. Even that was not enough for the president. Before long, he started a military buildup in Vietnam. Eisenhower probably would have gone to Vietnam, read Ho Chi Minh the riot act, and placed American soldiers on the border to avoid any further North Korean incursions. Instead, Kennedy laid the groundwork for the Vietnam War. It was a war that changed the trajectory of the American economy from that time forward.

In the aftermath of JFK's assassination, Lyndon Johnson's landslide, plus his political ruthlessness, permitted him to get just about anything he wanted. In short order, Great Society legislation, including Civil Rights and Medicare, became his legacy. Like JFK, LBJ was also enamored of the invincibility of U.S. military might. And, following the reduction in taxes

Economic Realities

during JFK's presidency, Johnson refused to raise them to pay for his adventures. We could have "guns" as well as "butter." Why not? The U.S. was still running trade surpluses with the rest of the world; a world not yet totally rebuilt after the mass destruction caused by World War II. Our industrial economy was still unchallenged from abroad. We were self-sufficient in energy and in nearly everything else. But now, with the costs of the welfare state and Vietnam War, our consumption began exceeding our production. In 1967, we were able to continue to stave off the Arab oil boycott initiated after the Six Day War, but not for much longer.

It became obvious, with the proliferation of money in foreign hands, that the U.S. could not possibly redeem all that currency with gold at $35 per ounce. In fact, gold on the London Gold Exchange - set up to trade on the eventuality that the U.S. would one day officially default on its pledge to keep the dollar parity to gold—traded at over $100 per ounce. In 1971, President Nixon did exactly that.

Almost immediately, prices in the U.S. began escalating. Then, in 1973, came the coup de gras. OPEC formed in the aftermath of the Yom Kippur War and raised oil price from about $3.50 to about $14 per barrel—almost precisely reflecting the rise in gold from about $35 to about $140 per ounce. Nearly overnight, prices more than tripled in the vital commodity and spread to everything else. We had double digit inflation. We also had economic stagnation as households grappled with utility bills that had risen five- or six-fold overnight. A new word—"stagflation"—was coined.

Technology, Longevity, Economy, Liberty

Our economic problems have been brewing since then. I place much of the blame on the failure of subsequent Republican and Democrat presidents to come to grips with the new reality and to rein in domestic overconsumption by insisting we keep our external trade in balance. That is, by insisting our imports be paid with exports and not by freshly printed and minted cash. From that time forward, neither economists nor politicians of either party have developed better methods of dealing with our impending balance-of-payments crisis and the resultant loss of American jobs. By the end of the '60s, much of post-war reconstruction was completed in Western Europe and Japan. But the dollar was still quite strong while most of those countries still had undervalued currencies. The Swiss franc was valued at about 25 cents, as was the deutschmark. The Japanese yen traded at 360 to the dollar. As a result, the cost of living in these countries, measured in dollars, was very low.

Likewise, European and Japanese wages were extremely low in dollar terms. I was earning a salary of about $10,000 in 1967 when I was sent to England on an extended assignment. My English colleagues were earning about 1,000 pounds, then worth about $2,800. Similarly, in 1970, I spent an extended assignment in Japan. My salary was approximately $12,000. My Japanese colleagues, however, were earning about $1,000 at the then prevailing exchange rate. But in most countries, including these, the cost of living in dollar terms was much lower than the cost of living in the U.S. In Japan, 360 yen bought more than a dollar did in the States. The same with

Economic Realities

four Swiss francs. Therefore, it made economic sense to buy products from those countries.

Remnants of the conditions prevailing at the conclusion of WWII, these wages and living costs created incentives for the U.S. market to absorb lower cost goods coming from abroad, particularly Japan. By the early '70s, this development was well on its way as low cost Japanese electrical products, such as the proverbial Japanese transistor radios, as well as mostly low end automobiles, began showing up in the States in noticeable quantities. So much so that, before long, the U.S. balance of payments suffered badly and left too many dollars in foreign hands. The original German Volkswagen Beetles, for example, also became ubiquitous.

The world noticed. Faced with choices to a) either severe austerity, tax increases, and other measures designed to reduce consumer spending, or b) letting the dollar float, President Nixon chose the latter. A decade of double digit inflation was ushered in. It severely and permanently eroded the value of the dollar at home and abroad.

The additional burden caused by advances in longevity exacerbated this trend. Let's do the math of an aging population. People began living longer and are now living until an average age of about 80. That means they will be on Social Security and Medicare for about 15 years. So now about 60 million people collect these benefits each year at about $18,000 for Social Security benefits per person plus another $15,000 for Medicare. This results in an expenditure of about $2 trillion, which will only be getting bigger.

Technology, Longevity, Economy, Liberty

At last count, the total welfare bill from all sources—food stamps, Medicaid, direct payments, etc.—was an additional $0.6 trillion. The total of these payments, $2.6 trillion, comes to approximately 16% of our Gross Domestic Product. This hardly seems sustainable to me. But what can be done? The left cries, "Tax the rich." The right cries, "Balance the budget and stop coddling the idlers."

Both arguments miss the point of what is happening. Maybe some additional taxation on high earners is justified. But the rich do not have nearly enough surplus wealth hidden in their vaults to close the gap between government revenue and spending. Most of the wealth of the rich supports the private economy, so that amount of additional taxation will come at the price of economic growth. On the other hand, there is a deficiency of jobs available for those of working age. Each year the percentage of working age people dropping out of the workforce grows greater. Add that to the many who are already retired, plus the baby boomers who expect the country to honor the commitment it has made to their well-being in their later years.

The numbers do not work. Personally, I am not a fan of printing money and running permanent deficits, the only solution that central banks everywhere have put into place. The current fancy term is "quantitative easing." The Federal Reserve and other central banks have taken to fund their countries' debts—internal and external—by purchasing government debt with money they conjure up out of thin air. If you say that is legalized counterfeiting, I couldn't contradict you.

Economic Realities

I fear that so-called Keynesian Economics, piling up more and more debt, cannot last much longer. When asked if he could predict what would happen in the long run, author of this economic plan, John Maynard Keynes, replied, "In the long run, we are all dead." Whether this story is apocryphal or actually happened, it is, nonetheless, fundamentally true. Even if it can work for a long while, eventually, it will collapse under its own weight. And the human costs are high. It creates an environment where an ever greater proportion of the population becomes dependent on the government for relief, thus creating a burden for those in the population still contributing to its growth.

Who can say when the bubble will burst? And who will be there to pick up the pieces when we finally come to realize that something new is necessary? In fact, Keynes himself never envisaged or advocated perpetual deficits. He favored balanced budgets over each business cycle, deficits during recession to stimulate demand, and surpluses during strong economic growth to keep the economy from overheating. Present day "Keynesians" are misusing Keynes' concepts to lend authoritative credence to perennial deficits, something he never advocated. Nor did Keynes ever advocate fiat currency (the printing of money backed by nothing). His idea of deficit spending was for the government to issue bonds to be purchased by individuals and organizations that had the wherewithal for such purposes. He never suspected that central banks, including the Federal Reserve, would resort to quantitative easing and become buyers of last resort, as they have in recent years.

Starting in the early '70s, inflation became rampant in this country, reflecting the rapid devaluation of the dollar following Nixon's decision to let it float. The currencies of our trading partners skyrocketed against the dollar. Scarcity of labor resulted from exports to the U.S. and caused inflation there as well. But, as noted earlier, their currency, relative to the dollar, also rose in value. So, the same 360 Japanese yen could then buy $3's worth of goods from the U.S. instead of the decade's earlier $1's worth. But, because of the severe dollar inflation during that decade, the U.S. buyer still had an incentive to buy items from Japan. What cost $1 to produce in the U.S. in 1970 cost $5 or $6 to make ten years later, but the cost was only $3 in Japan. This decline in relative value of currencies with our trading partners dramatically affected the dollar price of oil, particularly after the OPEC cartel formed following the 1973 Yom Kippur War. OPEC countries had virtually no middle income blue collar class. All the oil wealth went to the royal families. As a result, there was no inflation there that resulted from Nixon's abandonment of gold. But the royal families felt the pinch of inflation from other countries as prices rose for goods purchased abroad. When the time was ripe, using the war as an excuse to extract a penalty for the west to favor Israel, unilaterally they more than quadrupled the dollar price of OPEC oil, from $3 to $14 a barrel, pretty much in line with the escalation of gold price after it no longer was pegged to the dollar at $35 per ounce and allowed to float.

The resulting revaluation of many Western European currencies and the Japanese yen against the dollar eventually created a semblance of wage and price parity in those countries

Economic Realities

compared to U.S. prices. But, Nixon made another historic move during his presidency. He visited China and gave them access to our market. It took a while to develop, but this one action completely changed the equation in ways that trade with Western Europe, and even Japan, did not.

In Western Europe and Japan, much of the benefits of global trade benefitted the middle class. Even if their income had not gone up at all in their currencies, they would have risen three- to four-fold in dollars. The results of such improvement were palpable. Standards of living in these countries approached and even exceeded those in the U.S. But, with such a huge population and after 20 or more years under severe communism, China had been so poverty stricken that the low wages prevailed. China had, and still has, a limitless supply of cheap labor and a mandarin class not yet willing to distribute the wealth in any other way than that is beneficial to only them, a small minority. As a result, Chinese currency could be kept low and the entire world's economy became particularly distorted.

Let's do a thought exercise with currency. Suppose country "A" still has the same prices and wages in "country A dollars" as they were in the late '60s. Country "B" has present prices and wages. In Country A, gasoline would still cost 35 cents per gallon. A nice house, manufactured there, could be bought for $25,000. A nice car, also manufactured there, for $3,000. Under those conditions, a good income would be $10,000 and a great one would be twice that. Country A would be quite prosperous, wouldn't it? People in Country B with present prices would rush to buy products made there. Next, imagine that the productivity of Country A is such that it could fulfill much of the needs of Country B while fulfilling all its own needs. What would happen? Country A dollars would quickly grow more valuable than Country B dollars. One way to look at it would be to say that Country A dollars had appreciated. Another way to look at it is to say that Country B dollars had depreciated. These statements are equivalent. The residents of Country A will then have a huge trading advantage for products they sell to, and the few products they wish to buy from, Country B.

In the real world, that is precisely what happened with several of our trading partners. Over the past 50 years, our prices have increased nearly tenfold, but prices in their own currency, for example yen prices in Japan or franc prices in Switzerland, have only doubled. That has been a boon to the economy of those countries and particularly the elderly, who have seen far lower erosion of their currency than the elderly of this country.

Here is an example of what might actually have occurred during the '70s for a retiree, such as an auto worker retiring from General Motors in 1970. Let's say he was earning $10,000 per year and his fixed pension from GM was, say, $7,000 per year. In addition, he began receiving $3,000 in Social Security benefits. Fast forward to 1980. That same retiree is still collecting the fixed $7,000 pension and Social Security was paying maybe $7,000 or so. Together, his income was $14,000, but the cost of living went up six-fold, so his 1980 $14,000 income only bought what $2,300 bought in 1970. In 1980, this guy is in trouble. Fortunately, he owns a home

Economic Realities

worth maybe $70,000 in 1970 and is now worth $150,000 in 1980 dollars. He can use that to augment his income, but he had better not live into his 80s. The money would all be gone and he would have to appeal to the government. That is precisely what has happened. With federal assistance, state and local governments set up Medicaid programs and other welfare vehicles to help people like the one in my example. People like our GM retiree became wards of the state after the state confiscated much of his wealth through the mechanism of hyperinflation.

Now imagine another scenario. Country A produces much of the products Country B consumes, but has an almost unlimited supply of low wage labor—nothing to even cause moderate inflation there. Then there is no price escalation in Country B for goods received from Country A. Without doing a thing to prevent it, inflation stops in Country B and prices even threaten to fall. Why? Because low-skilled people are thrown out of the workforce in Country B and are reduced to subsistence, living on the dole, either with low wage part time employment or without employment at all. Demand diminishes for Country B residents, particularly those unemployed or underemployed, which means there is abundance of supply but scarcity of demand.

This has been happening in the real world since about 1980, both here and throughout the rest of the developed world. Country B is any country in the developed world. Country A is China. Under a situation such as this, prices tend to stabilize, or even fall, not only for imported goods, but also for goods and services produced in Country B. Deflation should be a natural result. You might see this as what is needed to restore equilibrium, which is how I see it. But there is a strong unintended consequence. Falling prices favor lenders and hurt borrowers. The impact would be incredibly painful to many, particularly those who have leveraged themselves to great wealth on the premise of ever increasing prices. For them, because the financial interests have created an economy based on debt, this "deflation" would be disastrous.

Even relatively average income people have existed on debt for way too long. Financial institutions, aided by the Federal Reserve, have created an incentive to spend and borrow, rather than save and lend.

That is the result of distorted Keynesian economic thinking, whereby the economy is driven primarily by consumption (demand), not production (supply). Frugality, a trait associated with an upright life, has been discouraged in the new economic order.

However, we all need to save for the time when we are no longer working and have to rely on our accumulated wealth to comfortably live out our retirement years. Unless we do so, sooner or later, we will all become wards of the state. Keynes never intended that his demand side theories would lead to permanent deficits and the need for central banks to continuously print money, precisely because there are so many dependent upon government money to survive; particularly retirees and the permanently unemployed who have neglected to save.

Today's interest rates offer little incentive to save and much incentive to borrow. So the charade continues.

Economic Realities

Furthermore, for many, the thought of deflation is frightening. It will have a negative impact on the perceived wealth of the majority in the short run. Nobody in office wants to deal with so much suffering. So the government is dead against policies that will result in falling prices. The media presents deflation as something to be avoided at all costs. In fact, there is such a fear of deflation that its opposite, namely *inflation,* has been touted by the Fed as desirable. The Federal Reserve has been actively promoting a 2% inflation policy for us. For the saver, this amounts to a confiscation of 2% of his wealth each year! This eats up a full third of the wealth of any retiree—particularly those like me, with fixed pensions—over the course of his retirement. Participation in the stock market becomes almost mandatory, despite its substantial risks. Those risks can be minimized, but only if some laws regarding participation are changed to limit speculation and leveraged buying. I'll discuss this further in a later chapter.

What is needed is an end to permanent deficits in our domestic and foreign accounts. I would tackle our foreign accounts first. Much of the country's debt, both public and private, can be placed on our perennial balance of payments deficits. Loss of jobs in goods producing industries to low wage countries bent on keeping their exchange values low in relation to the dollar, has contributed to a massive increase of dependency in the U.S. Each year, the number of able-bodied people no longer in the workforce, therefore not even counted as "unemployed," has grown. This is not a new phenomenon and it has become worse under both Republican and Democrat administrations; particularly escalating in the

Technology, Longevity, Economy, Liberty

21st century. Since 2009 alone, the workforce nonparticipation rate has grown approximately six percentage points, totaling an additional nine million people or so of working age who are not working, yet are not counted in the unemployment statistics. If counted, the number of unemployed in 2016, particularly in jobs paying breadwinner wages, is greater than it was in 2000. **In other words, our economy is on a death spiral in plain sight.**

Meanwhile, our country is sitting on a huge glut of gas and oil. So much so that prices have plummeted, even with the severe restrictions on the growth of the industry placed on it by the present administration. What we now have is an industry potentially capable of meeting all our domestic needs and still being able to export our surplus into the world market. The production of crude oil is greatly restricted, particularly offshore and in Alaska. Much of this potential production is high quality, low sulfur, and light—qualities that enhance its value in the marketplace. Even if we can produce only two million more barrels per day for export—a conservative estimate—we could reduce our deficit by half with China and create a great number of high paying, long lasting breadwinner jobs. Export of natural gas, a commodity we now have in great surplus, can close the other half. China needs both and it needs access to our market. Shouldn't this be done and wouldn't it be a win-win?

If we balanced our trade, we could once again peg the dollar to the price of gold. This will be discussed later in the book. But, with this, I do not see any need to run deficits. We have run them for so long that many of our institutions assume inflation will continue. Those of us on Social Security expect a yearly raise. Most employees expect regular salary increases, even though their value added (productivity) has not increased.

There was a general strike in France in 1968. I was on assignment there and witnessed the impact. The workers demanded an immediate across-the-board raise. De Gaulle obliged and ordered a 5% raise for every worker in the country. One year later, the French franc was devalued by that same 5%. Coincidence? Of course not. Money alone is not wealth, but rather it is a means of exchange of wealth. If anyone, De Gaulle should have known that. In 1971, he was the immediate catalyst for President Nixon to officially take the dollar off the gold standard. De Gaulle wanted gold for his dollars, but the dollar had become a fiat currency, not much different from the French franc, which had been devalued so many times that a new currency had to be introduced. One hundred old francs were replaced by one new franc and many of the old timers still reckoned prices in their old currency, a disconcerting practice to a foreigner such as I.

The only *real* wage increases are based on productivity increases. That is a function primarily of technology. More economic means of production leads to lower unit costs per unit of labor. These wage increases do not lead to inflation, but we have been living in a world of inflation for so long that we have almost forgotten what it would be like to live in a non-inflationary world.

CHAPTER 7
POLITICAL FAILURES AND POLARIZATION IN BOTH PARTIES

I was born during President Roosevelt's third term to parents who were first generation immigrants. They were born in Eastern Europe and brought to America by my grandparents just after World War I. Living in cramped quarters, they were poor, uneducated, and hard working. However, they had enough to eat, eked out their livings, loved their adopted country, and made tremendous sacrifices for their children—sacrifices that could never be properly repaid. Of course, they never had any notion of such.

FDR was their man. He was a god to them, and for good reason. He created the basis for the welfare state, instituted Social Security, and reinforced collective bargaining, partially leveling the playing field between the rich and the rest of us. By the end of World War II, as prosperity finally settled in, few

Technology, Longevity, Economy, Liberty

challenged his achievements, not even big business. The era that I call "Corporate Socialism" came to be, mostly as a result of the New Deal policies instituted in the '30s and the U.S. ascendance after WWII in the '40s. Labor and management fought itself to a standstill and good manufacturing jobs were abundant in steel, coal mining, auto production, oil, and gas. The country prospered more than anybody could have expected.

But, as is often the case, trouble was brewing. Human beings apparently do not know how to handle a good thing for very long. The avant-garde became restless and lashed out at the conformist, anti-artist and anti-intellectual mood of the country. They directed their anger at the rear guard, the Midwest "Babbitts," who returned the animosity, worried that these so-called "liberals" who were not content with the economic gains made were really closet communists in league with Communist Soviet Union and were now showing their real colors. Both sides were right, but wrong. The culture war, started in the 1950s with the Beats, Ginsberg, and Kerouac, egged on by authors such as Norman Mailer, and roused by the anti-Communist witch hunt led by Joe McCarthy, had begun.

The Republican Party, already thought of by intellectuals as having nothing of importance to say, began taking on the mantle of paranoia, seeing the "left"—any Democrat—as a closet Stalinist. The right pushed the Democrats in that direction and the left dutifully obliged. It took a while but by the time of the Kennedy assassination, the poisonous polarization had begun to settle in.

Political Failures and Polarization in Both Parties

The assassin, Lee Harvey Oswald, defected to the Soviet Union four years prior and became an outspoken Castro supporter. Yet the event was depicted as caused by a culture of hate that had arisen in the country. Nobody in the media would look at the facts and declare it what it was—an attack by a confirmed communist on an anti-communist president. The assassination became the clarion call for the internecine political warfare that both sides fomented. No longer was the Republican Party the party of entrenched big business that had accommodated itself to FDR's New Deal reforms. Eisenhower himself, such an accommodated Republican, was seen as a traitor in some quarters on the right. On the left, Eisenhower was the boring clod who brought the nation to a state of dull conformism.

The Democratic Party slowly evolved into the party of the "oppressed" classes. The party of FDR gave up its positive mission of seeking justice for the working man, since that was largely already accomplished, and began to see the U.S. in negative terms. James Piereson writes:

"When they looked around, liberals in the 1960s did not see progress: instead they saw blighted cities and ghettoes, a despoiled environment, and rampant bigotry and discrimination. White Americans had enslaved blacks and committed genocide against Native Americans: they had oppressed women and tyrannized minority groups, including Japanese Americans who were interned in the camps during World War II. Americans had been harsh and unfeeling toward the poor. In our greed, we had ravaged the earth and were consuming a disproportionate share of the world's resources. The United States coddled dictators and violated human rights out of an irrational fear of communism. With this bill of indictment in hand, liberals began to recast the reform ideal, turning it from an instrument of progress into one of punishment." [7]

I was a 20-something when this occurred and I admit I was somewhat taken in by the rhetoric of the times, though not nearly as hostile to the country my parents taught me to love. My hard work was already beginning to be rewarded with an important job at Esso. Like many at the time, I was influenced by the rock music of the era, especially the words of Bob Dylan, a great spokesman of that period. *"Something is happening but you don't know what it is. Do you, Mr. Jones?"*

Lyndon Johnson assumed the presidency upon the assassination of JFK in 1963. The following year, he handed Barry Goldwater the biggest shellacking any candidate for the presidency ever had. He was in a position to accomplish just about anything he desired. And most of that was positive. His "Great Society" agenda included Medicare, welfare reform, War on Poverty, and sweeping civil rights legislation. But he also inherited his undoing—the looming war in Indochina that would develop into a full-fledged debacle, creating the greatest schism in U.S. history since the Civil War. That schism has never been quieted and still exists today. Even more serious than that, Johnson financed all his Great Society legislation and his hugely unpopular war with debt. That was the beginning of the long slide into the nation's indebtedness and

Political Failures and Polarization in Both Parties

polarization that we experience today. It has taken that long to develop.

While there were many on both sides of the political aisle that agreed that civil rights and poverty issues needed, finally, to be addressed, the extremists, left and right, made the most noise. Right wing racists declared LBJ's well-intentioned reforms were communist-inspired. And leftists obliged by fanning the flames declaring any opposition to the enacted reforms as signs that the country was becoming fascist.

In 1967, Esso offered me an assignment in England at its refinery in Fawley. I jumped at the chance to live abroad. The Vietnam War was already in high gear and poisonous anti-Americanism was in the air. Given the climate of intellectual opinion in the states, I can now appreciate, if not the origin of such venom, then at least the tacit approval of opinion makers in the U.S. I was taken aback. Of course I could see that the United States was far from perfect. But it is one thing to criticize one's country from within and a far different thing to witness denunciation of it when abroad, particularly from a country for which so much blood and treasure had been so recently expended. Newspapers deliberately depicted our slums as far worse than they were. I know because I lived in a notorious one as a youth. I began defending America in a way I never would have thought of doing at home.

Another Esso family lived close to us and we became fast friends. Branchy was a Cuban émigré who had fought in the Bay of Pigs, imprisoned there, and finally ransomed by the U.S. who gave the Cubans a fleet of buses and other items in return for the release of all prisoners. Branchy was a fierce anti-Castro

Cuban. I obtained a much different perspective of things from him.

We returned to the States just before the Democratic Party's ruinous election in August or September 1968. By then, race riots blighted many American cities, such as Watts, Detroit, and Newark. Assassinations of Martin Luther King and Bobby Kennedy, so soon after JFK's assassination, convinced the most far left that a vast conspiracy was propelling the country to a fascist - neo-Nazi even - future. The convention in Chicago was marred by street violence never before seen at a political event. Witnesses saw Mayor Daley's cops using their night sticks on the mob, who were screaming, *"The whole world is watching."* It was. Yet, the whole scene ended up badly for the radicals within the Democratic Party. Hubert Humphrey, LBJ's Vice President, the spokesman for the worker wing, won the nomination.

Perhaps this nearly two year sojourn in England allowed me to gradually comprehend the profound change in the message of the Democrats from, as Piereson describes it, progress to punishment. From the late 1960s onward, the Democrats began their abandonment of the white working class, turned their fury on them, and instead embraced identity politics.

The radical wing, represented then by George McGovern and Eugene McCarthy, was defeated. In the general election, Humphrey lost to the despised Richard Nixon. But the radical elements in the party had made great progress and set the stage for their slow takeover of the party.

Political Failures and Polarization in Both Parties

By the time Nixon became president, the national debt and our overseas debt were both beginning to explode. Rather than reversing the trend, he made it worse. The United States was still on the gold standard and, at least nominally, committed to redeem currency at the rate of $35 per ounce. By 1970, the rest of the world realized the U.S. could not make good on that commitment. The London Gold Exchange market was already trading gold at over $100 per ounce. Foreign leaders, notably Charles De Gaulle, began demanding gold in payment for the dollar reserves. Nixon's fateful answer was to renege on that commitment and let the dollar float, setting in a decade of double digit inflation. By the time things began straightening out, it was the 1980s and the dollar lost more than 50% of its value against major currencies (the Swiss franc, the German deutschmark, and the Japanese yen).

Following the disastrous presidency of Jimmy Carter, under whose watch Iran became a world threat, President Reagan set the stage for significantly lower tax rates in the country with a minute reduction in spending. In fact, he increased military spending significantly, which, while it was instrumental in helping end the Cold War and the collapse of the Soviet Union, added significantly to the national debt.

Under Reagan, then Fed Chairman Volcker sought, successfully, to quench inflation by driving up interest to unheard of levels. While it succeeded, it set the stage for the Savings and Loan crisis, during which about one-third of the Savings and Loan institutions failed. These institutions were forced into risky investments in order to pay the double digit interest rates needed to attract savers. The first crisis, double digit inflation, begat the next one.

In 2001, President George W. Bush came into office and reduced taxes once again just as President Clinton and Speaker Gingrich managed to get the deficit under control and run some surpluses. By then, the Republican orthodoxy was to lower taxes first and balance the budget later. They called it "starve the beast." But politicians in both parties wanted no part of such starvation. Their political clout (and electability) derived from the ability to provide undeserved goodies to their constituents.

President Bush repeated the deeds of President Johnson. He also fought the Iraq and Afghanistan wars while reducing taxes. Plus, he added a brand new Medicare entitlement program for prescription drugs.

During this time, both parties helped create the real estate sub-prime lending crisis leading to the Great Recession we continue to reel from today. Fought by the Obama administration with trillion dollar deficits, there still seems to be no relief in sight.

So, no, I cannot let the Republicans off the hook any more than I can excuse the Democrats. The Republicans talked the talk but, since Eisenhower, they have not had the courage of their convictions of such talk; their over-the-top devotion to "the Gipper" notwithstanding.

Political Failures and Polarization in Both Parties

CHAPTER 8
THE FAILURE OF THE WELFARE STATE

Jack Kemp liked to call himself a bleeding heart conservative, because he sympathized with the *aims* of the so-called "Welfare State" but not with its *methods*. Conservatives have, in general, used the term "bleeding heart" as a pejorative and that has hurt their message. Liberals reflexively shut out arguments from the right and think of them as uncaring and greedy.

I understand what Kemp was up to with his verbal jujitsu. He was standing up for conservative ideas and wanted to clarify that the "tough love" suggestions he was making had, at least, some chance of improving the lot of those in poverty. He said what should have been obvious—that the War on Poverty had failed miserably in its stated purpose of ending poverty. In fact, it can be argued that systemic long term poverty, extending

Technology, Longevity, Economy, Liberty

into the second and even third generation of dependency, reached epidemic proportions early on and has remained there.

Trying to cure present day poverty with the tools and rhetoric of the early 20th century is a fool's (or charlatan's) errand. It is easy to demonize people who are well-off by insisting their wealth comes off the backs of the impoverished. It is far more difficult to do anything about the entrenched poverty, assuming those doing the demonizing even want to do something about it. I may be wrong, but I have my doubts.

Poverty remains where it was when President Johnson initiated his War on Poverty. Why? There can be only two explanations. The first is that the people in charge are, indeed, fools who refuse to accept the necessity of change in order to permit those displaced by automation or the global economy to become independent. The second is that the people in charge are, indeed, charlatans and like things just as they are because they have a constituency of people totally dependent on the very programs that keep them from said independence. Remember the sign in that New Orleans taxicab? When you've got them by the balls, their hearts and minds follow. After all, independent people do not need to be "taken care of" by the state. Those who are hopelessly dependent just can't see that. Putting the blame on the well-off is easy. Creating an environment where those displaced can function independently is far more difficult. It is a challenge most politicians shrink from or simply dismiss because it against their self-interest.

The War on Poverty was supposed to eliminate conditions like those that existed in the Brooklyn slum where I grew up

The Failure of the Welfare State

in the '50s. It was no picnic. As kids, we heard horror stories about fights between black and Italian gangs with fancy names like the Gay Cavaliers or the Gay Valentinos. We also heard rumors that the thugs used high school shop class to produce "zip guns," but I never saw one. The only drug we ever heard of was "reefer." There were times I had to defend myself from thugs (mostly black, but also white), and got badly beaten up once or twice, but I never once feared for my life.

Now, 60 years after I entered high school and 50 years since landmark civil rights legislation and affirmative action were introduced to put an end to black misery, the problems in inner cities make anything I encountered growing up in Brownsville seem ridiculously tame by comparison. Nearly every day, we hear stories of young black victims, often innocent, caught in the crossfire, perpetrated by other young blacks, who by my lights, are victims as well. Things could have been different.

President Johnson awarded Daniel Patrick Moynihan, then a noted sociologist and not yet a Senator, the job of advising on what should be done to help blacks rise out of their poverty. The Moynihan Report, "The Negro Family. The Case for National Action," called for a massive social effort to reduce the profusion of fatherless homes, noting that that, more than any other single factor, ***including the prevailing racism,*** created the biggest schism between blacks and whites.

When the report was released, the usual loudmouth politicians and academics accused Moynihan of racist stereotyping, blaming the victim, etc. Johnson, the consummate politician, shelved the report. That one ill-conceived action of political cowardice changed the landscape and condemned countless kids in future generations; some to death and even more to wasted lives. Moynihan was no racist. He understood that the nation as a whole was culpable and urged that something be done at the national level to repair the damage at the source. Instead, we got excuses and halfway measures. Even today, we are reluctant to face this problem. Only the most courageous blacks talk about black-on-black crime using those words. Guilt ridden whites hide behind weasel words like "inner-city violence."

Fifty years later, this "inner-city violence" is far worse than it was when Johnson rejected The Moynihan Report. Its results are as clear as day. Consider this recent example. New York City has three magnet technical high schools; Bronx Science, Stuyvesant, and Brooklyn Tech. These schools provide exceptional technical training for about 3,000 students entering them each year. I attended the latter, received a full scholarship to the Cooper Union, and had a great career, as did many others from various ethnic groups from similar economic circumstances. In 2015, a grand total of eight black kids in all of New York's five boroughs passed the entrance exams for admission to Bronx Science. That's a crime. But what's the solution? The new mayor suggests lowering the standards further. But lowering standards and not owning up to the real problems is what got us to where we are today.

Isn't it time to acknowledge the failure of that approach? Isn't it time to shed the fear of being called out as racists by the race hustlers in the media, academia, and politics who have a vested interest of placing blame for the failure on anyone

The Failure of the Welfare State

but themselves? It's way past time to dust off, update and, most importantly, implement the Report and stop burying our collective head in the sand. Currently, three times as many black kids grow up in fatherless homes. Polite people, not wishing to sound accusatory, look the other way and self-righteously blame the "legacy of slavery," contenting themselves to ignore the shocking murder rate in the inner cities. The "legacy of slavery" argument fails to explain the explosion of fatherless homes in the black community that has occurred since the initiation of programs in the War on Poverty. Or, for that matter, a similar explosion of fatherless homes in the white community since then that has also had severely negative effects. That may sound prudish and out-of-date, but it is the truth.

I admire the courage of some in the black community who have stood up to the strong chorus coming from the race hustlers who have a vested interest in feeding the hostility many blacks feel toward whites. Maybe their message will begin to resonate. Here is an excerpt from a recent essay by Thomas Sowell:

> "(N)owhere (is the division 'us against them') more clearly expressed than in an attempt to automatically depict whatever social problems exist in the ghetto communities as being caused by the negligence of whites, whether racism in general or a 'legacy of slavery' in particular. Like most emotionally powerful visions, it is seldom, if ever, subjected to the test of evidence.

The 'legacy of slavery' argument is not just an excuse for inexcusable behavior in the ghettos. In a larger sense it is an evasion of responsibility of the disastrous consequences of the prevailing social division of our times and the political policies based on that vision over the past half century.

Anyone who is serious about evidence need only compare black communities as they evolved in the first 100 years after slavery with black communities as they evolved in the first 50 years of the welfare state, beginning in the 1960s.

You would be hard pressed to find as many ghetto riots prior to the 1960s as we have seen in the past year (2014–15)…

Murder rates among black males were going down—repeat DOWN—during the much lamented 1950s while it (sic) went up after the much celebrated 1960s." [8]

Sowell goes on to confirm Moynihan's ideas about the relationship with family strength and a properly functioning community. He notes that the poverty rate is in the single digits in black families where a father and mother are both present.

The deterioration of the black organic family, either encouraged or ignored by the strategies instituted in the wake of Great Society policies, has led to disastrous results for the blacks these policies were meant to cure. Any well-meaning reformer should recognize this and not be blinded or led to

The Failure of the Welfare State

inaction for fear of being labeled a racist (if white) or "Uncle Tom" (if black).

And let's look beyond the black community. The Welfare State has encouraged, and thereby created, a vast culture of dependence in the country. Many conservative intellectuals like Sowell have pointed this out. Jack Kemp and others consider themselves to be "bleeding hearts," genuinely sympathetic to the plight of those who are now caught in the web of dependency, brought about by the policies of those who purport a wish to help, yet continue to advance policies that do just the opposite. These conservatives are maligned for their efforts and their proposed solutions have difficulty finding the light of day.

The Great Society Welfare State solutions have failed. Every well-meaning person should admit it and take Dr. Sowell's admonitions seriously. Excusing the inexcusable is a disastrous evasion of responsibility. George W. Bush called such behavior "the soft bigotry of low expectations" effectively turning the racist charge on its head, back to people who claim to have pure motives but persist in avoiding responsibility for their inaction.

CHAPTER 9
THE FLAWED CONCEPT OF "FREE TRADE"

Lest I give the impression that I only fault the Democrats and the Great Society legislation for our economic and social ills, please let me state that I believe many actions and concepts emanating from the Republicans are at least as responsible for the downward and economic social spiral set in motion in the late '60s. After all, it was Nixon who abandoned the fundamental concept of a strong currency, backed by real wealth, and allowed the printing of fiat money in a desperate attempt to provide the appearance of prosperity while the country was facing double digit inflation. This led, first, to quadrupling of oil prices and then to the near total collapse of the dollar against other currencies. By the end of the '70s, large portions of our strong manufacturing base were disappearing. Conservative Republican orthodoxy lauds free trade, regardless of the long term consequences on employment opportunities, particularly in manufacturing. I recall hollow rationalizations in the '80s when we were told we were in a post-manufacturing era. Yet the Gipper twisted the meaning of manufacturing so much so that it was meaningless. According to Reagan, fast food companies, such as McDonald's, should be counted as manufacturers. That is how far afield conservatives have gone with the concept of manufacturing, trying to gloss over the loss of our industrial base. No, fast food does not replace the loss of domestic production of just about everything we consume, televisions, appliances, textiles, furniture, and even farm implements.

The way I see it, free trade is a positive if it leads to more employment and lower costs for both trading partners. It is far less of a positive if it leads to mass unemployment for one of those partners. Of course, if you are a beneficiary of lower prices and have not lost your job as a result of it, you may have a better opinion of free trade than if it was your livelihood that was threatened or eliminated. An economics professor at Harvard is certainly more likely to laud the benefits of "free trade" than a displaced auto worker in Flint, Michigan or a steel worker in Pittsburgh.

But, even if you are an economics professor at Harvard—especially if you are an esteemed expert—you should see what is just in front of your eyes. Since the '70s, our workforce has continually eroded. Each year, more able-bodied people below retirement age drop out. Since 1970, about 18% of that demographic has left and are no longer seeking employment. Nearly every year, welfare rolls, or other forms of

The Flawed Concept of "Free Trade"

public support, have grown. I wonder whether our esteemed economic gurus have taken the cost of such a burden on our economy into account in their calculations of the value of our free trade; trade which may be free but is also unfair in many cases. I doubt it. If they did indeed make such an observation, we would not be excluding that 18% from our unemployment statistics, would we? Nor would we be so cavalier about adding to our national debt to support our ever weakening economy.

Such deceit emanates from both parties as they try to create the best news about our faux prosperity, financed almost exclusively by both public and private debt. If that is not a prescription for disaster, I do not know what is. Yet, as I look around at the general population who seem to be oblivious to what is in front of them, I am perplexed. Neither party has the courage to face the ugly truth that we are on a death spiral.

In fact, as I see it, the ultimate failure of LBJ's Great Society legislation has largely been a result of the erosion of high paying "breadwinner" jobs in goods-producing industries. If those jobs had expanded in the '60s and '70s as much as they had expanded in the '50s, then maybe the failure could have turned into a great success. The way I see it, not only were white workers in Flint and Pittsburgh victimized, but inner city blacks in Chicago and similar ghettoes, now denied the jobs that have fled offshore, were perhaps victimized at least as much. So, count me in with Jack Kemp. I am also a bleeding heart conservative and have come to the conclusion that, while I sympathize with the goals of welfare state advocates, I do not think much of their methods. Nor am I a fan of corporate welfare, the crony capitalism, emanating from Washington, D.C., that dominates and distorts so much of our economy and benefits so few. What follows is a discussion of where we are as a result of this massive failure and a hint of what I think can be done to reverse the trend. It will take sacrifice, but I believe I have laid out a fair way to begin to tackle the triple whammy of automation, globalization, and longevity that has placed such an enormous burden on our economy, provoking sleepless nights for many of us as we worry that yet another major collapse—far worse than the Great Recession—is just around the corner. We need to act now to take steps to reverse the trend.

The Flawed Concept of "Free Trade"

CHAPTER 10
DROWNING IN DEBT

The United States Government is drowning in debt. The national debt now exceeds our Gross Domestic Product (GDP) and is growing at a frightening rate. Meanwhile, each year a greater percentage of the working age population has given up on finding employment whatsoever. It is not my intention to stigmatize those who have chosen a life of dependency over a life of productivity since most are victims of the system and may have made rational decisions given the options available to them. Rather, I place the blame where it belongs—on the officials who have created the mess by not dealing with any of the ramifications of their pronouncements and allowing things to fester from bad to worse.

The fact that so many people are choosing welfare over work is troubling. It is the direct effect of our global economy policies. Here I part company with many conservatives who see only the good in free trade but fail to see the negative consequences when it is unbalanced. Participation in the workforce by people in the working age population has been on a steady decline since the late '70s as many concluded they would be better off receiving public assistance. From 2008 to 2015 alone, workplace participation declined from about 65% to 62% of the able-bodied. That is about five million people who have dropped out since 2008. The general public is kept blissfully uniformed about this state of affairs as these people are not included in unemployment statistics. Both parties have been guilty of perpetuating this deliberate obfuscation. **If we are ever to escape the death spiral our economy is in, this trend must be reversed.**

Unfortunately, virtually nothing is being done at the moment to reverse the trend and there are serious, even calamitous, ramifications to its further neglect and accumulation. Running perennial deficits is supposedly a principle laid out by John Maynard Keynes, arguably the most influential economist of the twentieth century. But the reality is that running such deficits actually contradicts Keynes' message. Keynes believed in "priming the pump" with deficit spending in times of slack demand and/or low growth. However, he advocated running surpluses to retard overheated economies, thus removing surplus demand that leads to inflation. He believed in a balanced budget over any cycle—deficits in lean years, surpluses in fat years. Stating it that way sounds almost biblical. It is surely benign if followed as Keynes suggested. Rather, politicians, using only the deficit side of

Drowning in Debt

Keynes' admonitions, have succeeded in creating the illusion of prosperity for the country through the mechanism of debt, both public and private. We are managing our resources like a wealthy heir who has run through his inheritance but still has available credit. He keeps on spending as though that borrowed money will never dry up . . . until it does.

Our collective and personal credit will also dry up one day. When this will happen is totally unpredictable, just as was the case in the 1929, 1987, and 2008 crashes. Like me, many fear the result will be far worse than the Great Recession of 2008-9 or even the Great Depression. My fears, even greater than the economic implications, are the political ramifications. If a leader does not rise up to provide hope for the populace during periods of persistent turmoil, a tyrant surely will. It happened in the 20th century with disastrous consequences—whole cities bombed to oblivion and death camps. Nothing will convince me that it cannot happen again.

It's not that the problem of the debt is not discussed. It is, perhaps ad nauseam. There are some who insist my fears are unwarranted. Perhaps they are correct. But the government already dominates 25% of the country's Gross Domestic Product. Demands for entitlement spending will consistently increase. So, even if the rest of the government spending can remain constant, expenditures will continue to grow. More and more people will be totally or partially dependent on the federal government. Meanwhile, more state employees willdraw unsustainable pension checks from state governments.

Technology, Longevity, Economy, Liberty

Let's first examine the federal budget under a scenario where the budget increases are in line with growth, with the exception of entitlement spending, which will grow faster. More will drop out of the workforce due to automation and the global economy. Still more will retire and fewer will die. The deficit and national debt will balloon unless there is enough growth. In 2015, the national debt was over 100% of our GDP. Unless spending is curbed dramatically, this debt will continue to swell. Government spending is the key. Even if the federal government can keep the percentage increase in spending down to half of a percentage growth in GDP, the national debt can only be contained if growth exceeds about 3.5%. But, the same entitlement spending is causing high government expenditure, retarding GDP growth, which has been flat and hovering around 1% or less. This is a classic catch-22. The only remedy is less government spending and/or greater growth in the economy.

Ask any economist and they will tell you that growth in the economy evolves from only two sources: 1) more people in the workforce and, 2) a higher productivity (more dollars of GDP generated per worker) from the workforce. That is a tall order if we persist in seeing a steady decline in our workforce of able-bodied population choosing public assistance over work.

We have no alternative if we want to stave off a disaster. We must take action, not only to reduce the deficit, but to eradicate it and begin to run surpluses. I believe this can be

Drowning in Debt

done in a way that many would consider fair. I lay out my proposal in subsequent chapters.

Additionally, we must reverse the loss of jobs to whammy one, unfair foreign competition. I will also present suggestions on how to accomplish this. Perhaps, most importantly, we have to tackle the long range problems that arose, not because of whammy one, but as a result of whammies two and three—technological advances that have reduced the demand for low-skilled labor and those that have allowed us to live far beyond our retirement age. Technology can be our servant or our master. Its advance has been at breakneck speed over the past century and, undoubtedly, will continue to astound us. But our economic and political institutions have not kept up with that speed. If we wish to remain on the rails, reform in these institutions is mandatory, from the ground up, if necessary. Otherwise, technology will enslave us. I think the job can be accomplished. The polls are showing us that people are beginning to understand that neither party has served us well and to realize we're heading down the wrong track. At least, they sense something is wrong. Clinging to outdated political and economic ideas, both parties leave the populace clueless as to what can and should be done. What I lay out in future chapters represents my point of view. That doesn't mean I don't think they're infallible. Just the opposite. I hope that all the concepts I am about to discuss should be regarded, refined, and improved on, in the hope that somehow they reach the people with the power; not only to discuss them, but act on them. I throw the ball in the air for someone to catch. I invite you to throw a better ball back to me. The more feedback, the better.

Drowning in Debt

CHAPTER 11
TACKLING THE TRIPLE WHAMMY

It is not nearly enough to simply talk about our fiscal and social problems. We have to consider solutions. First, we need to throw useless names and the resultant name calling out the window. Our antipathy to one another is precisely what our political class feeds upon as we verbally assault each other rather than attack the real source of our problems and beneficiaries of the status quo. I have faith that we will find common cause with each other if only enough people come to understand how we got into this mess in the first place. Then, with understanding, we can insist on the changes needed to reverse the untenable situation we find ourselves in. Why? Because the case for change is riveting and a majority of people across the entire political spectrum believe that our country

Technology, Longevity, Economy, Liberty

is headed in the wrong direction. We need to tackle the triple whammy that has so distorted our economy.

Whammy One—we have lost a great, and increasing, chunk of our manufacturing sector to countries that have manipulated their currencies so there is no chance we could ever achieve trade parity with them. Whammy Two—automation has eliminated many jobs, mostly low-skilled, probably more than Whammy One. As a result of Whammies One and Two, we have experienced a steep drop off in the percentage of the working age population who are gainfully employed. It would be even worse if the payrolls of government at all levels were less bloated, particularly at the Federal level. Yet the people who are not contributors to the private economy have to be taken care of. I certainly do not dispute that the indigent have a claim on the public purse. What I dispute is whether public assistance is the best way to handle this vast and growing problem.

Whammy One—loss of our manufacturing—doesn't necessarily mean bringing the Apples or Microsofts of our economy back to the U.S. But it does mean leveling our playing field with the countries that engage in unfair currency manipulation. By far, we are China's largest customer and we have a huge negative balance of payments with her. The goods we buy from mostly U.S. based companies are paid for by consumers here. Low cost Chinese production, sold into a high cost market like the U.S., benefits these companies' shareholders who are, at the least, mostly upper middle class. The same is true for the effects of Whammy Two. Even more low-skilled workers have lost their jobs to automation than to

Tackling the Triple Whammy

countries with unfair trade practices. Robots are taking over large chunks of backbreaking labor. Productivity has increased steadily. However, this increase in productivity comes with a curse—the large overhang of redundancy.

That is one of the reasons the stock market remains high, but it is not an accurate reflection on the state of the economy here for a working class that has been displaced, who own very little stock, and therefore, are left out of the equation. That is a startling observation that needs to be delved into. If the working class owned stock in the companies that have sent their jobs overseas, in roughly the same proportion as their lost wages, they would no longer need public assistance. Think about that. All we need is to find a way to make that happen. "Lots of luck" is what most people say when I express these thoughts to them. Cynicism has taken over. Few still consider the U.S. as the shining house on the hill. This is where I make a leap of faith. I propose it can be done and I will outline the solutions. The people have the power to eventuate change if they choose to use it.

Even if we weren't faced with Whammies One and Two, we would still have Whammy Three to deal with—the longevity issue. As I've pointed out, people are now living two or more decades past their retirement age. Every one of them has a claim to the public purse. They have paid into the system and believe they are entitled. I'm not going to disagree. But the government has already spent the money it has collected for their retirements. The Social Security trust fund contains only T-bills, really just IOUs. That is a fact. The only way the government can make good on those IOUs is to raise taxes or print money. From recent experience, my guess is that they will take the latter course. Sooner or later, however, that dam will break and we will once again have runaway inflation. All that is needed is a revolt in China by workers demanding a living wage for the labor they provide to keep their kleptocrat leaders and their American collaborators living large. The government is making promises for the long run that it cannot possibly keep. Therefore, I surmise that balancing our budget is the necessary step to restoring fiscal sanity. I think this can be accomplished in a way most of us consider fair, even if the economy remains sluggish as I expect it will.

Our economy is totally distorted. We have the Federal Reserve, which has kept interest rates artificially low, encouraging increased oversupply of some commodities. Natural gas and crude oil production, based on the latest fracking techniques, skyrocketed, leading to lower prices for these commodities. Technological advances have continuously led to lower inflation adjusted prices. Yet, even with this downward pressure on prices, the Federal Reserve, counterintuitively, insists on manipulating the economy to achieve a 2% rate of inflation. This is beyond my comprehension as it leads to our labor force being less and less competitive in the world stage and more dependent on government intervention.

Like many others, I have a fixed dollar private pension and a second fixed dollar health insurance stipend. In the four years since my retirement, I have already seen an erosion of that health insurance stipend by about 15%. Over the course of my 20-year post retirement life expectancy, that 2% per year inflation figure amounts to a purchasing power erosion of 40%. That benefits my company. They will pay my pension in inflated dollars. But it is a breach of fiduciary responsibility on the part of the Fed to me. This scenario is far from merely theoretical. In Chapter 6, I took a look at how deep a hole a hypothetical 1970 retiree would have been in by 1980, following a decade of double digit inflation madness. Then, of course, Social Security benefits are indexed to inflation. So the inflation problem feeds on itself, creating ever greater deficits and more inflation.

The Social Security system has been called the "third rail" of political discourse, even though it is demonstrable that with today's payroll taxes that support it, most individuals would do far better in retirement if those same funds were allowed to accumulate in private accounts actually owned by those individuals, which I will demonstrate later in this book. The left has fought such "privatization" on the grounds that it would place those individuals at the mercy of Wall Street predators. That fear bears much validity. The markets have become too volatile. That volatility needs to be tamed before any privatization scheme could and should be acceptable to the general public. It has actually been government currency and interest policy that has contributed to that volatility of stock market boom and bust. The following are my ideas on what I believe would help. Let's start there and analyze both faults and fixes.

From at least the Great Depression on, it has been understood that leveraged speculation in the market can lead to market crashes. After the 1929 crash, new laws were enacted to minimize this leveraged speculation. Margin accounts were limited to 50% of the value of the individual's stock portfolio. More recently, however, options trading, put in place, permitted individuals to control stocks with as little as 10% cash value in those stocks. Derivatives were then developed that take the ability to control a stock with absurdly little money in the game. These changes have made the stock markets many times more volatile as they would be if the original law of no greater than 50% margin accounts were not superseded by margin and derivative accounts. Option and derivatives trading have effectively circumscribed that sensible law. Now, in particular, as more people than ever before are living their retirement with income from their IRAs and 401Ks, it is time to make changes to make the stock market more conducive to investment and less so to speculation. Gambling casinos are springing up everywhere for these speculators.

There is a reason people say they are "playing" the stock market. To too many, the stock market is treated like a gambling casino. People put money down, often highly leveraged money, and trade on volatility not necessarily related to the stock's fundamental, present, and future earnings potential. That leads to booms and busts. We have seen the result—overheated markets and dramatic crashes.

Now in particular, savings accounts are not an option because of low interest rates. Therefore, as most of our retirements are tied to the stock market, it is not too much to insist that the stock market should be for investment, not speculation. An investor should ask the question: "How much return will there be with this investment?"

However, the emphasis currently in the market is too great on price fluctuations rather than earnings. That is precisely the wrong way to view the market for serious investors. The market has crashed too many times, making people feel insecure. In an effort to avoid even worse crashes, the Fed and other central banks have driven interest down to a zero rate (ZIRP—zero interest rate policy) or even negative rates (NIRP) in an effort to prop up stock prices as a way of protecting investors from the ravages of ever greater crashes caused by the very speculation, particularly the highly leveraged variety, that has caused such action by central banks worldwide. In my opinion, this is faulty to an extreme.

Savers seeking a decent return on their bank accounts have been victimized to an even greater degree. They either must join the stock market, which, understandably, they wish to avoid, or accept a diminution of their wealth. In fact, in the long run, given the roller coaster ride that is the stock market, everyone who seeks a secure retirement—savers, shareholders, bondholders, etc.—remains needlessly insecure. Our economy is so distorted that a large swath of the younger generation, the so-called "millennials," many of whom cannot find jobs despite their costly advanced education, have given up on capitalism and are ready to embrace socialism. That would be a disaster. What should happen is the end of crony capitalism, that is, unfortunately, so pervasive today. Rather, we need the real free enterprise which has contributed so much to us as Americans and, by extension, to the free world. The crony capitalism variety results more from too much state interference than from too little.

The remaining chapters outline what I believe can be done to reverse our disastrous course that has resulted from the failure of our political and economic institutions to keep pace with our technological developments. This failure affects everything as it has reached epidemic proportions, not only here, but across most of the developed world. The effects of the triple whammy have led to shaky economies, growing dependency on the government, and unbridled private and public debt. This state of affairs has created bubble after bubble, leading to crash after crash, and unnecessary insecurity for too great and growing percentage of the population. To correct this will take sound leadership and an end to the political corruption that has fed into the cronyism that leads to prosperity for too few and dependency for far too many.

In the following chapters, I lay out what I think are commonsense suggestions to tackle the problems as I see them. If these suggestions were to be heard by those most powerful, there is little doubt they would regard them with scorn and derision. The less powerful may recognize their merit, but would claim, with some justification, that I am dreaming. Maybe I am. But if the potential solutions are not even discussed, how can there be any remedies?

I will address the following:
- Balancing the national budget and eliminating the debilitating debt hanging over us.

Tackling the Triple Whammy

- Reducing our overseas Balance of Payment to manageable proportions while at the same time creating jobs here in the U.S.
- Drastically reducing the uncertainties and anxieties of our retiree population caused by over speculation in our equities markets that affect their retirement accounts.
- Creating an alternative to the present Social Security system, strengthening it more than ever for the time when the millennials retire, thus avoiding the potential bankruptcy many anticipate.

CHAPTER 12
THERE IS A SANE WAY OUT

Many have been led to believe there are no alternatives to continuous deficits, low growth, and creeping confiscation of wealth, primarily of the elderly and others living on fixed incomes. Politicians and economists on the left who have ravaged Keynes' theories make those claims, while the right presents an opposite case. The fact is, the red ink flowed when they were in power as well and nothing was done to reverse job loss to China or the crony capitalism that spawned that policy in the first place. During the presidencies of Reagan and both Bushes, deficits were endemic and the super-rich thrived as the Fed rigged markets in their favor. To me, the Republicans' recent promises to have balanced budgets sound hollow.

Technology, Longevity, Economy, Liberty

Only during the Clinton presidency, with a super strong (some say "overheated") economy, limited military spending and a strong push from the newly elected Republican majority Congress, was the federal budget somewhat contained. I say "somewhat" because the Social Security and Medicare trust funds still needed to be raided to pay for the rest of government operations. Even then, non-entitlement spending exceeded income and entitlement income exceeded payout during those years. And the surplus was intended to fund future shortfalls, not present government operations.

Since the late 1990s, economic growth has been anemic and characterized by growing government indebtedness. We have been reduced to consuming far more than we produce. Fewer able-bodied people participate in the workforce every year, yet they consume nonetheless, financed by the government's printing press.

I can't believe that overconsumption here will lead to prosperity. Emerging economies, particularly China's, deliberately keep wages so low that their workers are not the true beneficiaries of the work they perform. U.S. trade policy supports this. A dictatorial minority in such countries with extreme wealth and power have become super rich. The relatively small middle class of professionals who run things benefit as well. The poor working class in China and elsewhere may be somewhat better off than they were before, but that does not excuse their exploitation. To a lesser degree, the same thing is happening here. The political class, lobbyists, and rent-seekers in the US– the beneficiaries of this state of affairs— attempt to justify this as "free trade." But, how "free" is it if the main beneficiaries are cronies of the political class in both debtor and creditor countries?

Free trade is only truly free if the rewards are mostly passed down to those who produce that wealth. Despite the Marxist sound of this, the concept is just as true when a strong believer in free enterprise, not crony capitalism, utters it. I believe in that sort of free enterprise. I prefer the term "free enterprise" to "capitalism". Individuals acting freely to better themselves do not necessarily require large sums of capital if they have skills or ideas they can exploit. It is arguable whether the political class in either party actually is motivated by a belief in that sort of free enterprise anymore. Perhaps that is why, over time, under administrations of both Republicans and Democrats, we've experienced a much weaker growth rate. Economic dynamism gets sapped out of the system when rent-seeking cronies of the party in power receive special tax treatment and subsidies. The right rails about too much welfare to individuals, but corporate welfare, crony capitalism, and rent-seeking is far more damaging to the economy. James Piereson discusses this in his new book, *The Shattered Consensus*.

> "The case was first advanced in 1982 by Mancur Olson in *The Rise and Decline of Nations: Economic Growth, Stagflation, and Social Rigidities*. In this insightful book, Olson tried to account for the 'stagflation' of the 1970s and the failure of Keynesian theories to explain it. He argued that democratic nations over time develop political rigidities that permit strategically placed interest groups to block breakthroughs in policy and to exploit political

influence in order to seize shares of national income that they have neither earned nor produced. These 'distributional coalitions' in Olson's terminology are organized around struggles over 'the distribution of income and wealth rather than over the production of additional output.' Often called 'rent-seeking' coalitions, they include cartels or trade associations, advocacy organizations, or corporations that try to increase the incomes of their members by lobbying for legislation 'to raise some price or wage or to tax some types of income at lower rates than other types of income.'" [9]

David Stockman makes a similar argument in his book, *The Great Deformation.* He accuses the Fed under most of the Chairmen since the Eisenhower days of policies that encourage speculation in the stock markets in favor of big money insiders such as Goldman Sachs and other well-connected investment bankers and financial institutions. He agrees with many on the left who believe they have too much influence and have succeeded in "deforming" the American economy to augment their own income at the expense of everyone else. That is quite a condemnation of the most powerful economic groups in the country.

Is it any wonder ordinary Americans are churned up, recognizing how their interests are being sold down the river to those who have undue influence in the corridors of power today? Imagine how bad it can get with the government taking control of an even larger slice of the national economy. The only way to avoid this and assure us all that we can enjoy the fruits of our labors and our investments is to begin to decrease the share of the economy occupied by the government and insider crony capitalists. Can it be done with so little pain that it can be accepted by the people? That remains the question. I believe it can, but only with some sacrifice in the short run.

There are two keys to sustainable growth that must be achieved in order to get our economy out of the hands of the rent-seeking cronies and back into our own:

1. We must balance our trade with the rest of the world, particularly China. The result? Increased employment here, thus reducing national budget deficit by eliminating of much of the welfare burden and receiving additional revenue from taxes of the newly employed.

2. We must begin the process that will lead to surpluses in the national budget and eventually eliminate the national debt. That will entail tackling the waste in government operations. But it will also require somewhat less generous entitlement benefits.

BALANCING OUR TRADE

The United States is in a disadvantaged position when it comes to world trade. This disadvantage does not fall equally on all of its citizens. Many in the diminishing middle class benefit from lower prices for many goods manufactured in places like China than it would cost for those same goods if they were made in our country. However, the class of those not skilled enough for the diminishing job pool bears the biggest brunt as they are permanently excluded from the workforce

Technology, Longevity, Economy, Liberty

and are almost entirely reliant on government welfare to sustain them. Go to any city, large or small, and you will witness young able-bodied people, mostly men, sitting idly and wasting their lives and talents.

We should do better. It would unfair of me to say we have not tried. The rise of community colleges, training many such people, has kept the problem from exploding. As mentioned earlier in the book, I arrived in Pittsburgh with my family in the early '80s. Pittsburgh, home of the once great U.S. steel industry, was coming unglued. Local steel mills all along the Monongahela River, the so-called "Mon Valley," were closing in droves, driving out an entire generation or two hardworking union men and women who, rightfully, felt betrayed. This was on the heels of a similar upheaval in Detroit and other auto manufacturing cities in the nation's Midwest.

Why this happened is easy to explain. During the 1950s, U.S. manufacturing reigned supreme. American manufacturers for most goods in the U.S. market remained unchallenged. Cars, televisions, refrigerators were all made here. Basically, all our consumer goods were made here, even our clothing and furniture. We even had a surplus of oil, requiring no imports from the Middle East. We were invulnerable . . . or so we thought. The quality of our products kept going down and our prices kept going up. Why? Because labor unions were winning unjustified wage increases without any increase in productivity. Any economist will tell you that this is a recipe for inflation.

The bubble burst around 1970. Imports began coming in; first as a trickle, then a flood. Prices dropped, but so did employment opportunities. The relative value of the U.S. dollar plummeted across the world. The Swiss Franc, worth 25 cents in 1965, approached parity in 1990. The Japanese yen saw a similar surge and nearly quadrupled in value against the dollar, while still allowing Japan to produce better quality products at lower relative cost. Neither management nor organized labor changed their positions in the face of this onslaught, resulting in permanent damage to both. Once at nearly 100% of U.S. consumption, U.S. auto production is now no better than 50%. And even those vehicles are equipped with parts made largely abroad. Other industries have fared even worse. Barely any apparel is produced here. The once bustling New York Garment District is gone; replaced by high-priced designers who make fortunes by designing here but purchasing in low-wage Asian countries. Refrigerators, televisions sets, washing machines—once produced here—are now produced there as well.

I could go on, but you get the picture. Besides, I hear you saying, "We all know what's wrong. But what can we do about it?" That will take much political will and skill. Correcting this problem will buck far more powerful obstacles and entrenched interests. Since the 1970s, so many CEOs, ostensibly backing the Democratic Party agenda, have nevertheless built their empires on activities contrary to the interests of U.S. workers. Walmart©, Microsoft, Apple, and Nike, to name a few, all rely on the U.S. consumer market for the lion's share of their profits while caring little about its citizens as producers.

BALANCING THE BUDGET AND ELIMINATING THE NATIONAL DEBT

The national budget is so far out of whack that any attempt to solve the deficit problem too quickly will surely lead to an economic disaster. Complex systems tend to crash if subjected to too large a change in too short a time. Change must be made in gradual steps. That is the key. I don't tolerate the hotheads who wish to make too big a change too quickly.

In my opinion, there is no expenditure so sacrosanct that it earns the right to be excluded from scrutiny. Both the left and right have their "sacred cows." Entitlement and welfare spending both need to be trimmed, as do government supported ventures that rightfully belong solely in the private sector. But so does the military budget and all manner of corporate welfare from energy company subsidies, including oil and gas companies, to suppliers of any type of renewable energy that requires government support for viability, including the support clamored for by the agricultural lobby.

Additionally, something is required to reverse the trend of steady decline in workforce participation by the 20- to 60-year-old able-bodied. Those people should be working and not be on welfare rolls. That will naturally reduce deficits. We need a proactive program to train these individuals and place them back into the workforce. To some extent, this happened in the '90s when Gingrich and Clinton worked together successfully. Their work has been undone in the Obama years, but needs to be revived. My goal, over the next ten years, would be to reduce this type of government dependency to a fraction, say, by 50% of what it is today.

There is a Sane Way Out

I made a calculation based on a strategy for long-term debt reduction. It requires gradual decreases in entitlement and non-entitlement spending. Today, in 2016, there are 59 million Social Security recipients and 150 million workers. As time goes on, the number of people receiving entitlement spending (Social Security and Medicare benefits) will increase, but the workforce will remain relatively constant. I estimated the increase in the number of people receiving such benefits going forward. In my calculation, each of those people would get Social Security benefits, but with a 0.75% reduction each year for ten years, on average, after adjustments for inflation. Rates stay constant after that.

For relieving economic burden at the low end of the incomes spectrum, I would weight those reductions so that they fall most heavily on people like me, well-off recipients (1.5% per year), less heavily on a middle group (0.75%), and not at all on the neediest. Additionally, I would aim to reduce long-term welfare dependency modestly, at 5% per year for the next ten years, and then take care of those most in need—those who truly cannot participate in the workforce for any reason.

The other part of my proposal is a 2% annual reduction of all other government expenditures for ten years. I would prefer if they were across the board barring favoritism to the sacred cows of left and right. I am quite confident that sufficient waste can be found in *all* budgets so that they can be trimmed by a mere 2%, at least in early years. A hiring freeze for non-essential personnel should be implemented as a way to jumpstart this.

If I assume even modest real (after inflation) GDP growth of 2% per year, this proposal would eliminate the deficit in about ten years, after which surpluses will be recorded. Beyond that, we would be running small but increasing surpluses and paying down debt. It will be a long, slow process and there will still be a residual debt until mid-century. After that, the country will be able to reduce its tax burden by about 25%. We will be able to afford our now huge entitlement budget. Our military budget will still be more than adequate and welfare will be under control.

Can this be done? Only if the majority believes it to be fair and no crony or special constituency gets an unfair advantage. It can only be done if the right and left stop squabbling and throwing the blame on each other and only if the right presidents are elected who are trusted by both sides. That is a tall order. The last such person to occupy the White House was probably Dwight Eisenhower, who rightly told us as he left office to beware of the Military Industrial Complex. I believe that such a man must come from the center, not from either extreme. I would prefer one who is a bit right of center, but who, like many on the left, also has a "bleeding heart" for the poor and dispossessed in the country. The following chart summarizes my calculations:

CALCULATION OF NATIONAL DEBT 2015–2050 ($ TRILLION)

	2015	2020	2030	2040	2050
BUDGET	3.7	3.7	3.9	4.3	4.5
RECEIPTS	3.1	3.4	4.2	5.1	6.2
DEFICIT/(SURPLUS)	0.6	0.3	(0.3)	(0.8)	(1.7)
NATIONAL DEBT	18.7	20.6	19.9	14.3	1.3

There is a Sane Way Out

Note that the budgets proposed minimize extremely substantial "belt tightening." If too much is done too quickly, the endeavor could not be managed. Note also that in the early years, the debt still grows. It will take at least ten years to balance the first budget. Let's face it. We all could pare a percent or two a year and might actually be better off in doing so. The average Social Security/Medicare recipient now receives approximately $33,000 per year in overall benefits, including health care. This amount would be reduced by only $250—$20 per month/per year for ten years and then remain constant. Perhaps much of this reduction can be recovered by decreasing unnecessary Medicare costs, especially fraud. In that case, the average Social Security recipient will feel no burden whatsoever.

I premised this exercise on a mere 2% increase in real growth per year and equal increase in government revenue. Some would call this growth anemic. Actually, simply reducing the ranks of the workforce dropouts will account for about a 1% increase in real growth. Naturally, any additional growth rate over the 2% assumed would improve on the numbers I generated. I also premised the exercise on the assumption of zero increase in tax rates. Increased government receipts in my calculation are totally a result of economic growth, anemic as I assumed them to be. I agree with Republicans that increased taxation should be avoided, but only if enough is collected to pay for government operations over time.

I mainly fault the politicians who have continued to promote counterproductive trade and welfare policies that paper over the problem and continue to feed abandonment of the workforce by an ever growing segment of our population. In particular, I fault politicians who promote:

1. Policies that create incentives for businesses to take their manufacturing overseas, particularly to countries like China, which has the power to keep wages low while, because of their totalitarian rule, having the clout to sustain that situation for the benefit of their small ruling class.

2. Policies that create incentives for people to rely on public assistance instead of finding work.

Since the Great Depression, politicians in this country have avoided the worst consequences of economic disturbances by expanding welfare during these turbulent times without expanding employment opportunities when the economy improves. Many of those who were displaced remained in that condition well after the downturns. Recently, I learned that obtaining welfare in Germany is conditioned upon looking for work and accepting it once found. Welfare recipients are bound to accept employment or lose benefits. They are permitted to turn down up to three jobs, but then must accept the next. That may work fine in Germany and may not work as well here. But it sounds to me like a solid idea. I also doubt if the laws concerning disability benefits are as loose there as they are here. In the U.S., an entire segment of the legal industry is engaged in representing prospective recipients of disability benefits. To its credit, there is no such industry in Germany. A system similar to the one employed in Germany would be a great help and would surely attract much public acceptance.

The problem is so endemic here that far more needs to be done. I am not in favor of a minimum wage, as I believe it is counter-productive and costly. The higher the minimum wage, the more incentive there is for private sector jobs to be exported overseas. This is obvious and widely accepted by those advocating a higher minimum wage. They argue that there are many jobs in retail, fast food, and housekeeping for instance that cannot be exported. I get it.

However, increasing wages for these low pay jobs ripples through the economy. People with greater skills, worth $15 per hour, for instance, demand to keep pace with those newcomers previously earning only $8 per hour who are now earning as much as they are. It is this ripple effect, an unintended consequence of the well-meaning effort to help the working poor, which will cause it to backfire as it always has. That is not an idle speculation. It has been going on since at least the '70s. Like most sacred cows, it is difficult to convince the advocates of ever increasing minimum wage that their policy is self-defeating.

When I started working in 1957 or so, the minimum hourly wage was $1. If that was a successful policy then, can anyone tell me why it hasn't been successful to stem poverty now that it has risen eightfold? The answer is that it contributes to the very inflation that leads to lower competitiveness of American labor and an ever greater abandonment of such in favor of lower rates abroad, should be obvious. But the issue has become a favorite of the class warriors in this country—those who fail to dismiss the fundamental fact that any act of government affecting the workplace creates incentives. Every nation gets the conditions its laws have incentivized.

While I do not favor the minimum wage, I believe that repealing it is a pipe dream. I also believe that, having been in place for so long, its abrupt cancellation would probably do far more harm than good. I, therefore, advocate leaving it alone for most workers. I would, however, welcome a well thought out policy to repatriate to the U.S. as many jobs as possible.

This may already be occurring. The shale boom has made the U.S. the low cost producer of gas. This has piqued the interest of global chemical producers to build facilities here. Much more could and should be done if only there weren't so much animosity on the left to this revolution. It's a no-brainer that production and export of liquefied natural gas to the Europeans should become an important industry. This will rid the Europeans of the hold the Russians have on their economy. Imagine the improvement in our balance of payments if, in addition, crude oil exploration and production is expanded and exports are once again permitted. The U.S. does indeed have the potential to become an oil exporter once more. A brisk market in the export of diesel fuel from U.S. Gulf Coast refineries has, also, come into being. This should be encouraged and expanded.

What I discuss here is not necessarily a completely well thought-out prescription to make American labor more competitive. But we have to start a dialogue somewhere. American wages are too high in the world market. That should be obvious. On the other hand, perhaps poorer workers in developing countries need the employment even more than our poor do. Wouldn't taking these jobs away create a worse world overall, including higher prices here and more poverty there? That is the next question I need to explore with the reader. How do we repatriate jobs without jeopardizing or reversing the amazing progress already attained in poverty reduction worldwide?

One way to balance trade is to restrict the dollar value of imports to the dollar value of exports. Can this work? And, if so, why hasn't it in the past? Let's start by examining our trade with China. The U.S. is the only country that has increased its imports from China from 2014 to 2015. Imports to most other countries from China have dropped quite dramatically. The Chinese continue to increase their reserve holding of U.S. dollars. That should concern us. It shows that we are consuming more than we are producing.

I would limit our imports from China to the exports they take from us and settle our balance in goods and services, not dollars. We may not produce consumer goods that could find a market in China or other developing economies. But we can produce food and energy for those markets. Oil and gas production can be greatly increased here if the government lifted the restrictions to production and export now foolishly in place. Furthermore, the mandate for renewable fuels should be lifted. That would free up the substantial production of corn and soybeans, now used for that purpose, to be offered in trade for consumer goods coming from China and other places. **I calculated the caloric value of those crops now grown for Renewables Fuel Standard. It can feed at least 400 million people.**

The supply side has performed well. Too well. There is too much idle capacity. But the demand side has not kept up. Too many people are without jobs and lack the resources to meet their needs, so must rely on the government to fill the gap. It is dangerous to our liberties to permit an ever growing segment of the population to become totally dependent on the state.

Please note: I do not begrudge the goodwill of those who wish to keep the most vulnerable of our country out of harm's way by supplying their needs through the welfare system. But goodwill, though necessary, is not sufficient to get the job done. Policies in place should not create incentives to avoid employment. If they are not working to motivate people to be independent of government largesse, it behooves those who espouse those policies to reconsider and change course. I understand and respect the goodwill of people with whom I disagree, but that understanding and respect is rarely reciprocated as too many on the left assume that we who believe in less government are the enemy of the working class who have nothing important to say.

To a large degree, because of an aging population, some public support will be inevitable as many people will rely too heavily on Social Security and Medicare in their post retirement years. But, that is no excuse for having a system that encourages able-bodied people below the retirement age not to find gainful employment and become as independent of the government subsidies as possible and net contributors to the economy.

The same is true for retirees. They deserve better and need more than near zero interest savings accounts, a stock market prone to frequent crashes, and an erosion of their wealth, in the form of inflation, engineered by the Fed. They even deserve

There is a Sane Way Out

a more lucrative retirement vehicle for the money they now put into Social Security and Medicare. Make the stock market into a more stable investment vehicle—instead of a speculative bubble-prone one—and that can be accomplished as well, as I will discuss next.

CHAPTER 13
NEEDED: EQUITIES MARKET REFORMS TO HELP MAKE RETIREMENTS MORE SECURE

The Federal Reserve interacts with our banking and financial institutions in a way that favors cronies and rent-seekers. Ordinary people are the victims. An increasing number of people are forced to rely on rigged markets to get by because they have no other secure source of income. Or—even worse—given the inability of many to obtain an independent income, they must rely on one form or another of welfare payments. Anyone, particularly if she is concerned about freedom of action and opportunity, who wishes to see what is going on, should conclude that such a state of affairs cannot end well. Call it statism, socialism, or whatever name you like: too much control over too many peoples' lives means far too much power in the hands of too small a group of people. That has never gone well in the past. And now, in the information age, where such a small group has an abundance of power, the danger is profound. Orwell's predictions seem to be coming true, just a few years later than predicted.

How can we reverse the damage? Ironically, I call on government to help here. Several steps need to be taken, which are undoubtedly controversial and probably can only be accomplished after a highly traumatic event. It might have been achievable in 2008-09 if the Republicans, the so-called non-statists, lived up to their ideals. But, as it happened at the time - and as it too often is - the Treasury Department was run by someone with strong financial and banking ties who convinced the president that these institutions were, in the now famous words, "too big to fail."

To my way of thinking, "too big to fail" marked what was the final death blow to a free enterprise economy and showed me that we were now in a managed economy favoring "bigness" instead of the freedoms needed to allow most ordinary people to reach their potential. I do not believe, as many of my fellow conservatives do, that such was the case or intention of FDR and his New Deal, or even LBJ with his "Great Society." I believe it is a natural extension of New Left politics embraced first by academics and later by the "progressive" wing of the Democrats who have now gained what seems to be total control of that party.

"Bigness" was once considered a threat to the country. At the turn of the 20th century, the power condition of the country was in the hands of a diminutive group of people. Rightfully concerned, progressives and conservatives enacted anti-trust legislation to do what they could to reduce monopoly

Needed: Equities Market Reforms to Help Make Retirements More Secure

power. The government then adjusted to diminish the power. Now, such oversight has gone missing. Big business and government have become closely aligned through lobbying and the sheer power of the "too big to fail" institutions that control the financial options of most Americans as they prepare for retirement and even more so after they do retire.

Despite the rhetoric, I have come to realize that big government actually prefers to deal solely with a few giant companies than with thousands of small ones. I am close enough to the activities in my industry (oil production and refining) to see how the largest of the firms in that industry seem to prefer enduring even severe and counterproductive government regulation to ensure their survival and bottom line, at the expense of the smaller, more vulnerable players in the field. The biggest players seem only too glad to agree to onerous regulations, convinced that the power of big government is here to stay, and knowing that the general public will pay the cost. If these regulations put the smaller participants at greater risk of going out of business, all the better for big industry.

A case in point was the recent attempt by the government to put a price on carbon emissions from stationary and moving sources. President Clinton floated the idea of a carbon tax during the first few years of his presidency in the mid-'90s. It was roundly panned, as was Hillary Clinton's Health Care Plan, and did not see the light of day. When the concept morphed into a Cap and Trade proposal in 2009, I was in charge of strategic planning and engineering for my firm, a smallish independent refiner. We were alarmed. The bill, as written, required every refiner to purchase these "carbon credits," and pray that we could pass them along to our customers. We pleaded, to no avail, for a carbon tax that could be posted on the pump as such, along with other taxes. That would, at least, level the playing field for both large and small companies and be collected when paid by the consumer. Because of the Clinton era debacle, the Democrats we talked to flat out opposed calling the measure the carbon tax it was. They preferred to create the impression that the oil refiners were to blame for the hike in the cost of transportation fuels that carbon credits imposed. Our early reading was that the cost of these carbon credits could exceed our profits and impose an enormous financial burden that many of us could not afford. Even those who could manage to finance these credits could end up losing money by not being able to recover the full cost at the pump. To big oil, this was no problem. In fact, the sooner we pesky little guys got out of the way, the better it would be for their collective bottom lines.

I do not have any such immediate experience with banking regulations. But I have heard similar stories about the inability of small banks to comply with the imposed onerous regulations. I have also heard the big banks are just as happy to deal with the regulations and simply let these "Main Street" banks fail.

The system is obviously rigged in favor of "bigness." Big business works well with big government. It can afford to comply with regulations small business finds burdensome and, in some cases, impossible to contend with. Ditto big banks.

*Needed: Equities Market Reforms to Help Make
Retirements More Secure*

Wasn't America supposed to be the Land of Opportunity? That was true when I was growing up. My poor working class family did well. So did my wife's family, who were much poorer. We succeeded in the private sector, thanks to the public and private generosity of the time. Yes, even then my father used to say, "It's not *what* you know; it's *who* you know." Granted, things weren't perfect, but if you're looking for perfection, you're on the wrong planet. It wasn't better anywhere else, that's for sure. But now we are faced with massive dependence on big government. I have been arguing that we have to rid ourselves of the yoke that has been placed upon us because of how the triple whammy—automation, globalization, and longevity—has been handled and has led to ever increasing dependency and ever decreasing independence.

In my youth, these issues, especially the looming problem of automation, were discussed, but little was done. Then, during the Reagan era, things began changing and, perhaps, we started moving in the right direction. I did not give President Reagan enough credit then, but now see that many of his ideas were directionally correct, at least in dealing with retirement issues. The IRA system was initiated under Reagan, creating tax incentives permitting working class people to acquire the wealth needed to finance their retirements. This initiative became imperative as old age pensions, the mainstay for the bulk of workers, began to disappear from the landscape, along with the companies that provided them, as globalization began shuttering much of American big business, creating the "Rust Bowl" in its wake.

Technology, Longevity, Economy, Liberty

While instituting the IRA system was a great achievement, it created an ugly unintended consequence—the rise of a Wall Street moneyed class that fed upon itself, had too much power, and was able to confer upon itself huge unearned wealth off the backs of its supposed beneficiaries. This has created an unsteady stock market scene, all too prone to periods of boom and bust. Since 1987, there have been at least three major stock market crashes, with surely more to come.

The problem is compounded by the simple observation that there is no other reasonable place for the ordinary saver to realistically go with his money. The Fed, reacting to each crash by driving down interest rates (now at near zero), has effectively eliminated savings as a vehicle for retirement planning. So, in a period of super abundance—gluts in energy, manufacturing capability, consumer goods, and food production—we poor working slobs are more insecure than ever. Nobody really knows what his real wealth is. A crash can occur any day, which would wipe out much of it.

So what do our authoritative economists say about the situation? "Don't worry." All this really means is that we should sit back and let the Fed print enough money and distribute it to all of the people our policies have hoodwinked and made wards of the state. Exaggeration? I think not. Is it any wonder ordinary people have lost faith in the "system"? It's time to rethink.

A good place to start is in the stock market. The market should be a place for investors to earn a reasonable return on their money. Unfortunately—tragically, in fact—it has been viewed more like a gambling casino than an investment

Needed: Equities Market Reforms to Help Make Retirements More Secure

vehicle. That has always been the case. The 1929 crash came as too many saw the market as a means of obtaining a quick buck, driving up prices to heights that were simply not sustainable. Even then, it led to a great economic disaster, when only a small percentage of the population was involved in stock market trading. Now, to a fairly great extent, a large proportion of retirees from the private sector rely on the earnings they can expect from their IRA portfolio of stocks and bonds. Many retirees from the public sector have pensions and feel a greater sense of security. But should they? Pension funds are, after all, also tied to the financial markets.

The financial crisis of 2008-09 was reputed to be caused by sub-prime lending, the misguided attempt by both parties to provide financing to allow just about anyone to own his own home. That is only partially true. The amount of money at stake was a tiny proportion of global commerce. But, the big banks—those labeled "too big to fail" that were eventually bailed out—leveraged those loans (assets on their books) into a far greater sum and, in turn, used those highly leveraged funds to take over many corporations. In the process, they transferred the proceeds of those transactions into their personal accounts. By financial sleight-of-hand, they managed legal thievery at unprecedented levels. Then, as more and more of these sub-prime loans defaulted, it created a domino effect and default in the collateral for which the big bankers were now on the hook.

The liquidity crisis could have been handled by letting those who took risks against those loans be wiped out and allowed to fail. But many years of crony capitalism had created an unholy alliance between occupants of the Treasury Department, the Fed, and those "too big to fail" banks. That is the conclusion reached by David Stockman[10] and others. The narrative is entirely convincing to me. Yet, I see some mitigating circumstances. Our retirement system, public and private, had become so inflated over the years that any substantial retreat would be greeted by the majority of ordinary Americans as a disaster, with their life savings wiped out. Never mind that those same ordinary Americans benefitted, at least on paper, from an inflated stock market with high price to earnings (PE) ratios. Inflated stock pricing created the "wealth effect," a phrase coined by Chairman Greenspan describing that sense of economic well-being not justified by reality. Those high stock market prices were unsustainable and eventually crashed, causing great anxiety to many of us.

Inflated stock prices allowed Wall Street royalty to get away with many shenanigans. Inflated valuations were seen as the salvation for the oncoming influx of baby boomer retirees who viewed the overvalued assets as a real indication of their wealth. It was not. Let me explain. Suppose a retiree's stock portfolio amounts to $600,000. He thinks he is that well off. But that depends on how much that $600,000 really earns. If the stock market is bloated and the PE ratio is 30, his shares are only earning $20,000 per year and his dividends are likely to be around $6,000. This guy is fooling himself that he is well off. If he takes out more than 3% of that per year, he will go broke much sooner than he anticipated. In fact, any portfolio that only earns $20,000 is not worth much more than $200,000 over the long haul. That is why investors looking at

*Needed: Equities Market Reforms to Help Make
Retirements More Secure*

financing their retirement should focus primarily on earnings and steer away from any strategy that makes them try to time markets. Timing markets is for speculators and, lacking Fed intervention by manipulating interest rates, losses would be as prevalent as gains for that class of people.

Therefore, speculation in a market that is meant to be an honest vehicle for financing the real economy should be heavily discouraged. Yet the Fed has played along with Wall Street speculation for a long time now. The result has been one bubble after another. The winners are the hated 1%, making the rest of us the losers.

It's hard for me to believe the people responsible for policies that inflated the value of those assets did not know what they were doing. So I will state what I believe is the problem. Because of its history, the U.S. stock market has been more of a vehicle for speculators than investors. The big players like Buffett "buy low and sell high." The emphasis is on buying and selling, not on earnings, the real underlying value of the stock as a source of income.

The model does not serve the income investor too well because, at any given time, the value of a stock may be severely deformed because of speculation. The professionals gloss over this problem and tell us to look at long term performance. These advisors have a point. Long term trends must reflect the long term returns of the underlying asset. However, there can be a sustained slump in a company's asset value that has little or nothing to do with the performance of that company. Why? Because investors and speculators are playing in the same league, with rules written by speculators who do little or nothing to help the overall economy. **The speculators should confine their betting to the numerous gaming casinos that have sprung up across the country, where the real odds should be at least as good if the Fed did not use its enormous power to prop up equities markets prices by manipulating interest rates and buying up government debt.**

I have been thinking long and hard as to how to improve the situation for investors and remove what I consider unnecessary anxiety involved in being forced to play ball in the stock market. Many, if not most, would prefer putting their savings in a safe bank account paying a decent interest rate and living off the account.

Take, for example, the case of a couple, age 65, of ordinary means, each earning $30,000 and now wishing to retire on an income of $50,000. First of all, they have to worry about inflation robbing them of 2% of their wealth every year. Why is that a good thing? I don't know. Ask Janet Yellen of the Fed. So, let's do the math assuming zero inflation. They probably will qualify for about $18,000 each for Social Security. This leaves a gap of $14,000 per year. To be safe, assuming they both live to a ripe old age of 95, they will need about $215,000 if they can be assured of a 5% return. Now, of course, that is impossible to do with a savings account or with bond ownership. In order to handle an inflation rate of 2%, they will need to save $271,000 or cut their budget down by $3,000 annually.

But, since a savings account is off the table, they are forced to put something like that amount into stock funds. For the

Needed: Equities Market Reforms to Help Make Retirements More Secure

first few years, they make out better on paper, earning 20% for three years. Then the market tanks and their funds lose all of their 20% per year inflated value, and remains at that low for five years. Worse things have happened in the market.

This couple is in a hole and that assumes Social Security remains solvent and pays the full present rate, adjusted for inflation; a risky assumption. Sooner or later, there will need to be an accounting that will force the government to rein in entitlements along with all other spending. It is a mystery to me that it's not happened yet. As I outlined in Chapter 12, I advocate reducing benefits for recipients by about 7-10% on average, over a ten-year period, graduated with well-off recipients taking up to a 15-20% hit. That includes me. I am willing to put my money where my mouth is, so that the least prosperous take no hit at all.

Forcing everyone into the stock market creates anxiety. When an individual invests in a series of companies, there is always risk involved. Any of them could go out of business or, at the very least, experience reduced profits. But the extreme fluctuations in the market can swamp that level of risk in any given period of time. A risk adverse investor can confine his investment to blue chips—which have withstood the test of time—and be content with that average return of 6 or even 7% or so. A more aggressive investor will look to find the next Apple or Microsoft. He will make out much better if he is successful. That is all part of the free enterprise system. But that system has become so distorted in the stock market that even those conservative blue chip investors have many a sleepless night as the market fluctuates at a far greater rate for even those shares than is justified by the ups and downs of their respective earnings. The present stock market model still reflects the pre-IRA model, with the speculators calling the shots. This creates too much anxiety. **The bulk of ordinary investors look only to get a decent return from the EARNINGS of their investments. Speculators play the market based on the PRICE of their holdings, which are not "investments" at all. They are the equivalent of chips in a poker game.**

Investors want calm markets, which move according to the real earning fundamentals of the shares of stock involved. Speculators care nothing about honest fundamentals. They feast on rumors and upheavals having nothing to do with earnings. Investors invest their own money. Speculators running hedge funds in the big Wall Street houses and banks rely on super leverage, sometimes above 20 to one, and when the leverage works against them, use their great political influence to get the Fed to bail them out. **It is long overdue for stock markets to be reformed in a manner that favors investors and discourages speculators, particularly those highly leveraged hedge fund speculators.**

There are many measures that could be put into effect to discourage speculation in the markets, even though, given human nature, there will always be the lure of the big buck that will keep gambling in the market as a way to hit it big. But, any diminution in such activity is a long term gain for the vast majority of investors, driven out of savings accounts because of near-zero interest rates. Perhaps the most potent would be to eliminate any leveraged buying.

Needed: Equities Market Reforms to Help Make Retirements More Secure

After the market collapse in 1929, measures were put into place to severely eliminate excessive leverage. Those rules, limiting margins to 50% of the value of shares held, are still in place but have been made irrelevant by the advent of options trading and the even more virulent derivatives trading. These forms of trading, along with short selling, instantaneous access to information, and "automatic trading" have created a whole new level of instability in the market that does not appear to impart any benefit to the economy as a whole. Additionally, it creates a level of anxiety for the entire population of retirees who only want a decent return, six or seven percent, on their investment to finance their retirement years, especially after they have put away savings over their entire working lives. Speculators have no special right to gamble in these markets. Let them go to any of the hundreds of gambling casinos available to them across the country.

I further believe that minimizing the impact speculators have on the market is not enough to reform the concept of ownership in the U.S. economy so that it is a decent place for retirement incomes. The need will grow ever greater as retirees form a growing proportion of the population and use the earnings to finance their needs after they leave the workforce and are no longer drawing payroll checks. **Retirees need to be assured they can tap the earnings that their ownership of shares should entitle them to.** Let me explain.

Assuming that the Generally Accepted Accounting Principles (GAAP) accurately represents a company's real earnings after taxes, then that company should, theoretically, be able to pay out all those earnings to its shareholders. So what if, by law, that company is compelled to distribute at least 75% of those earnings to its shareholders? If so, shareholders would be less interested in fluctuations of the price of their stock and more interested in the return they get in the form of dividends, which is what they should have already been focused on for their retirement income.

Here's an example. Company A shares sell for $50 and have earnings of $8 per share. Company A is obligated to distribute 75% or $6 per share to its shareholders. That's okay if the company chooses to reinvest only that $2. But most companies seem to prefer using more than 25% of their earnings for reinvestment for other purposes. Say Company A is such a company and wishes to invest 50% of its earnings. What would happen then? Well, the company can provide the shareholder a choice. If the shareholder wishes to receive only 50% of earnings, they are given additional shares of the company's stock, representing the earnings they leave in the company. The shareholder who wishes to take the full 75% of earnings stays with their now somewhat diluted initial shares.

Next year, their earnings will be less than the shareholder who decided to reinvest part of their earnings with the company. Both investors get what they want. Retirees may want the full 75% distribution. Younger people saving for their retirement may choose to reinvest the full 75%. The company, of course, is free to offer additional stock to the general public as a means of financing its reinvestment plans, or it can issue bonds. Everybody gets what they want, unlike the "one size fits all" nature of today's markets. **Shareholders are entitled to the earnings from their investments and should be free to**

Needed: Equities Market Reforms to Help Make Retirements More Secure

take those earnings or reinvest them. Even if the company's management were totally trustworthy, it should not be free to make that decision for them. Sadly, I believe that many companies have managements that are not trustworthy enough. How many of them award management with compensation packages that bear no resemblance to their performance?

I know that this proposal may sound radical, but I don't think it is. I do not feel that CEOs have the right to withhold money from those shareholders who wish to receive their share of the company's earnings. But I recognize that getting legislation passed to fix this situation will have extremely low probability. Therefore, as an alternative to a law requiring such action, small shareholders may need to organize and force their companies into adopting these standards by voting at annual meetings.

In summation, I offer the following recommendations:

1. Restore rules that eliminate leveraging practices favored by speculators. Abolish options and derivatives trading altogether and limit margin accounts as well.

2. Require companies to state earnings by GAAP standards and distribute 75% of those stated earnings as dividends. If 25% of earnings fall short of the company's requirements for reinvestment, they should issue more stock. Each shareholder can decide whether he wishes to take the cash dividend or receive more stock in its place. Or, absent binding federal law, shareholders should organize and force corporations to require such action.

With these two reasonable reforms, I believe most of the speculative fever will be removed from the market and relocated into the gambling halls where they belong. There is really no excuse to allow speculation to play games with stock market valuations, particularly if they cause bubbles that produce a "wealth effect" causing investors to believe they are wealthier than they really are and make poor choices that could jeopardize their financial future. These "get rich quick" schemes, so prevalent here—the downside of capitalism, really—must be eliminated to the greatest extent possible. So many people will live to a ripe old age. It behooves us to protect them from hustlers and crooks, particularly those who masquerade as financial wizards who lead them down dangerous paths.

Lacking the upheavals that have taken place with regularity since the late '80s, the stock market should reflect the continuing health and strength of the U.S. economy. Let's look at how a conservative long term estimate can keep a normal wage earner comfortable in their retirement years. Suppose a high school grad decides to forego college and opts to become a skilled worker, say an auto mechanic. He begins working at age 18, earning $18,000 per year as an apprentice. Over time, his skill set and value increases. Each year, his income goes up by a modest 2% more than inflation. What if, instead of paying into Social Security, that individual earns 6% per year on that money, with savings they accumulate tax-free for 45 years? At 63, rather than earning more, he wishes to retire. By now, he is earning $43,000 (inflation adjusted) and his savings have grown to $817,000 (also inflation adjusted).

Needed: Equities Market Reforms to Help Make Retirements More Secure

Here is a summary of his earnings and savings over their working career:

AGE	INCOME	SAVINGS	RETURN $/YEAR
18	$18,000	$2,700	$160
30	$23,000	$57,000	$3,400
45	$31,000	$230,000	$13,700
63	$43,000	$817,000	$49,000

He can now retire on that 6%, which will now earn him about $49,000. He is earning more money after taxes and savings than he earned while working. Social Security is eliminated for him and his entire generation. And when he dies, he can leave his estate to his children who now have a running start to their retirement goals. Call it privatization of Social Security if you wish, or "Capitalist Socialism," widespread ownership of capital by individuals (people, lower case), not collectively (upper case, The People). Wouldn't that be a great improvement over the entire concept of collectivism?

I realize the above calculation is theoretical and that in any given year there can be a reversal of fortune. That fear is what the proponents of keeping today's system sell to the general population. It is a scare tactic that should be easily expelled. Consider first, that the 6% figure I quoted represents a fair estimate of what a conservative position will produce over the long haul. Compare it to the present Social Security system where that individual pays into the system at the same rate. He will have to wait until he is 66 or 67 or even older to obtain full benefit, which will be around $19,000 per year, will disappear upon his death, and can be reduced or even eliminated by government order. To me, the proposed benefits of privatization outweigh the liabilities to such an extent that it is a no-brainer. Privatization is far better for such a person. Also it would put an end gaming the system that benefit freeloaders by using the loopholes and taking advantage of the system by increasing contributions in just a few years before retirement. Privatization would put an end to that unfair practice as well.

*Needed: Equities Market Reforms to Help Make
Retirements More Secure*

CHAPTER 14
DISLODGING US FROM DEPENDENCY

There are approximately 25 million able-bodied adults who have stopped seeking work. That is what automation and the global economy has wrought. A few are idlers, but the vast majority would love to have a productive job in the private sector instead of having to rely on the indignity of living on the dole. In fact, more than indignity, many of their lives are in danger. There has been an uptick of deaths in the population of white males from alcohol and drug abuse, poisoning, and suicides.[11]

In my profession, I have seen many such people. Having spent the past 25 years working in rural Rust Belt western Pennsylvania, I have witnessed these unfortunates up close and personal. Many can do almost anything mechanical working with their hands or with machines. I have hired several to work

Technology, Longevity, Economy, Liberty

for me, performing multiple tasks I cannot, or choose not to do by myself. Many have had drug or alcohol related problems. In the typical old industrial town where I have worked for many years, most of the employers of this group of people have gone away—some are out of business and others are abroad.

Fortunately, western PA continues to produce gas and oil, albeit in relatively small quantities, so there are few true ghost towns. Of course, many once thriving towns would benefit from a strong boost through more employment. Other parts of the great Rust Belt are much worse. The situation has impoverished two generations of formerly proud middle class blue collar workers throughout the northern Midwest where countless blue collar industrial jobs, mostly union, have vanished. Some fortunate workers have found employment by moving south, often doing similar work at lower pay. But, as cost of living tends to be lower as well, they can live just as well as they did with union jobs up north. Unfortunately, many of these jobs have also disappeared. The luckiest ones saw the writing on the wall in time to move to oil producing states where the pay is best, jobs are relatively plentiful, and the cost of living is relatively low.

The trend toward loss of jobs is part of the fabric of our society. This must be reversed. Well-meaning conservatives talk about free trade as if it were the Holy Grail. If China wishes to trade their goods for a bunch of IOUs, they say, the loss is theirs, not ours. But is it? Millions of able-bodied people in the nation may differ. And, if those who have no choice but to vote for a statist party that redistributes wealth as a means of supporting them, given their inability to find work, how can

Dislodging Us from Dependency

conservatives expect them to listen to their pronouncements about the benefits of "free trade?" Their arguments fall on deaf ears if nothing is ultimately done to reverse the trend of loss of decent breadwinner jobs to automation and globalization. No, they refuse to listen and I don't blame them. To wean them off dependency, we must address their legitimate needs and develop an economy that meets those needs outside government handouts.

That is not to say the government doesn't have a role. Conservative orthodoxy states that government is best when it governs least. That may be true, but that does not mean that government should stand by as one group, the wealthy, exploits another group, the poor and/or weak. In the era of the Robber Barons, laws were instituted by conservative as well as progressive statesmen to level the playing field somewhat between these groups. First, there was anti-trust legislation, then wages and hours, then other public welfare measures. To be sure, perhaps the pendulum swung too far the other way with minimum wage legislation and laws favoring unions that had the effect of driving U.S. wages so high they were no longer competitive on the world scale.

When the pendulum did swung the other way, U.S. businesses took their manufacturing offshore with the idea of repatriating goods made back home. When Ford Motor opens a plant in England to build cars for the English market, that is a good thing for both England and America. But, when Frigidaire moves its manufacturing to East Asia, and produces refrigerators for U.S. consumption, that is another thing altogether. And it's not good. Those refrigerators should be utilized in East Asia to benefit the workers there. Unless, of course, they are not the right fit for the Asian market. Instead of IOUs to the state, those foreign workers should receive something of equal value from the U.S. economy that will improve their lives. Perhaps with higher wages there, we could provide those workers means to fill their energy or nutritional needs far better than they are currently. That additional wealth could go a long way toward significantly improving the lot of the Asian workers who toil and get little benefit as the products they produce are not theirs to enjoy. It would also create more employment opportunities here in the U.S. That would be a win-win and produce the free and fair trade we conservatives supposedly advocate.

A similar argument can be made to address the problems caused by automation. High wages created great incentives to have robots and other high tech machines replace human workers. This trend has been going on since the beginning of the industrial revolution, but has accelerated over the past 40 years or so. The problem would not be as severe if ownership of the shares of companies producing our wealth were more widespread so that, for example, a displaced assembly line worker owned sufficient stock to offset the wages he lost when a robot came in and made his job redundant. More widespread stock ownership would go a long way toward the goal of easing the dependency on the government when people lose their livelihood entirely or have to take a job with lower pay.

That should be the long term goal of any reforms initiated. I have attempted to lay out what is required to accomplish this.

Dislodging Us from Dependency

It will not occur overnight and anyone telling you otherwise or asking you to join his revolution to accomplish "social justice" will lead you to disaster, particularly if that someone wished to expand government many times greater than its already bloated and corrupt present state. This is not mere speculation.

If the trend to an even greater expansion of government is to be avoided, which is necessary to provide for those idled by the triple whammy, things must change. The present state of affairs is unsustainable, so the sooner, the better. Improving employment opportunities here and creating an environment allowing for and encouraging widespread ownership of capital are necessary game changers. Reining in government spending is also needed. Most will agree that discretionary spending budgets are bloated and should be pared down gradually. Nobody can convince me that a mere 2% reduction per year cannot be shaved off the budget simply by eliminating waste and corruption if there is a will to do it. Similarly, even individual entitlements should be able to be cut by an average 0.75% per year, a mere average of $250 per individual, if the waste and corruption in the Medicare system were finally tackled in a meaningful way. And, if employment opportunities can in fact be improved, the task of reducing and eliminating the federal deficit would be that much easier to accomplish.

Renegotiating some of our trade agreements to improve our export situation is needed to increase job opportunities here. If this results in a 5% per year positive swing in the welfare budget, we may be able to actually balance our budget in ten or so years and pay off our enormous national debt in perhaps another 15.

What is preventing us from doing this? I believe there is an incestuous relationship between our government officials and the most powerful in the private sector that is preventing such action. The most obvious such relationship is between the Federal Reserve and the largest lending and investment banks—those deemed "too big to fail." These financial institutions were caught red-handed during the last sub-prime mortgage meltdown that thrust us into the great recession from which ordinary Americans are still reeling.

Market watchers are obsessed with actions by the Fed that creates incentives for speculation. Such actions drive market valuations that have nothing to do with any individual stock's underlying value. If this obsession with price were replaced by more interest on those investments as income producing vehicles, then restoring interest rates to their rightful place would be much more acceptable by those ordinary investors relying on income from those investments.

That can only happen if these ordinary investors are able to rely on a steady stream of dividends reflecting the earnings their shares actually have produced in the securities they own. Right now, that is impossible for a variety of reasons.

1. Earnings reported are not necessarily those calculated by GAAP (Generally Accepted Accounting Principles.) Why that is allowed is a travesty. All publicly traded companies should be required to report GAAP earnings along with any other criteria they wish.

2. No minimum share of such earnings is required to be distributed to shareholders. This needs to be changed. I advocate that at least 75% of the GAAP earnings per share calculated be distributed to shareholders. These shareholders would then be free to retain these earnings or reinvest them in that company or any other company they choose, as they likely would do while saving for retirement. After all, it is their money, not the CEO's or the Board of Directors', who, after all, should be servants, not masters, of their shareholders.

3. Dividends are treated as ordinary income while capital gains are taxed at 15%. Dividends should be treated the same as capital gains. Corporations already pay taxes prior to such distributions. If capital gains are taxed at 15%, so should dividends be. Conversely, if dividends are taxed as ordinary income, so should capital gains be. Favored tax treatment for capital gains over dividends makes no economic sense but creates an incentive for shareholders to accept meager dividend distributions.

If these changes were implemented, speculation in the market could be greatly reduced and would represent a significant improvement in the elimination of insecurity, creating a far greater trust in our equities markets. The average person would be better off and it certainly would not hurt those less risk averse, those who are willing to invest in new ventures and products to enhance their wealth. Plus, it would also be welcomed by those who wish to put their resources in less risky steady earners.

If these changes were implemented, I foresee the possibility of gaining general acceptance in privatizing social security, which would be a much better deal in the long run than relying on its continuance in its present form, as I've outlined earlier. The changeover will require a generation to accomplish because payments from present workers are now needed to fund those already on Social Security. If privatization were to occur, it would have to be implemented in such a way that people in the middle of their careers still receive a prorated portion of benefits from the old system while paying into the new system. That is a bit tricky, but it can be accomplished without too much of a problem. It may take a few years of extra government expenditure before the benefits of the new system will reduce the overall cost of the programs. But, with more people working as the result of better trade agreements, the government would be in a far better position to deal with implementing more solid and secure vehicles for the population in general. This can be accomplished by reducing the amount of government intrusion into our lives and relieving the threat of an even more intrusive government, a more socialistic one, becoming attractive.

My dreams go even further. If I had the power, I would run the government as a business, with a capital budget and an expense budget. This can only work if the capital budget creates income for the government. For example, suppose we wish to run an electric grid from Texas in high wind country to California where that wind power would be consumed. The

Dislodging Us from Dependency

government could charge private users a fee to send power across that grid, perhaps making it possible to harness that wind at competitive pricing. The government could then issue bonds against that money-making facility and return, say, a 5% dividend on those bonds. Or, if the government invests in high speed rail, it could do the same; each venture with a separate bond offering. Every year, these expenditures could come up for vote in Congress so, yearly, we would know how much money can be collected by the sale of real interest bearing bonds, not zero interest ones. After paying out dividends, the surplus could then be applied to the expense budget. We would know, annually, how large a tax burden would be required to handle those expenses. Our government can work for us again rather than our working for it. What a concept.

CHAPTER 15
CLOSING ARGUMENTS

I have tried to honestly assess the extent and origins of our present economic malaise. I have also attempted to lay out a long range strategy to reverse course and set the stage for recovery, by looking realistically at the root of our problems; their causes and cures. Let's summarize.

The state of our economy bears no resemblance to the economy we had in the fifties under Eisenhower. At that time, nearly everything consumed in the U.S. was also produced here. Our economy went through mild boom and bust cycles, but there was general prosperity and a thriving middle class made up largely of unionized workers in the manufacturing industries. Now, despite the rhetoric about how productive our manufacturing sector is, few are employed in it and very few of our consumer goods are, in fact, produced here. This is the result of automation and the globalization of the economy. High wages here have made the American labor force, and those of most first world countries, uncompetitive.

Exacerbating this trend is the fact that third world countries, notably China, have opted to manipulate their currencies to keep their wages low. In my opinion, that is a perversion of the concept of fair trade, as it robs low wage earners in third world countries and fails to benefit the low-skilled workers in first world countries, as many are unable to find jobs that pay breadwinner wages. The only people to benefit are the relatively affluent in first world countries and the corrupt state officials in third world countries.

This perversion has led to massive deficits that have grown since 1970 and are now endemic. The U.S. economy has consumed trillions of dollars more than it has produced, which has created massive internal and external debts. These deficits have deformed our economy almost beyond recognition, and have led to unprecedented periods of boom and bust.

Both internal and external debt needs to be addressed, but the astronomical amounts need to be reduced gradually in order to preclude a severe crash. The eye must focus on the prize—namely a balanced economy. I believe it can be accomplished by mid-century, but not without pain. The necessary suffering can be endured and will fall most heavily on the more affluent, but not by increasing taxation. That is self-defeating, as it creates a disincentive to invest. My proposal for gradual reduction of entitlement and discretionary government spending accomplishes that without tax increases,

Closing Arguments

but patience is needed as it will take until mid-century to clear the deck.

I advocate an eventual return to a gold standard for clearing relatively small amounts of external imbalance. Of course, if imbalance of trade is too great, a gold standard cannot be made viable. That is why I recommend limiting imports to something close to the value of exports. As long as wages in this country are too high, there will be few consumer goods produced here to fill the bill. But we have food and energy resources that can be used if our political system allows them to become available for that purpose.

We can easily produce extra oil and gas sufficient to reduce our balance of trade by half if those in power were less obsessed with demonizing the fossil fuels industries or nuclear power plants. And we can provide more food to the world, as well. The caloric value of just the ethanol and biodiesel we use in our fuels, produced primarily from corn and soy beans, are sufficient to feed at least four hundred million people. Why not offer those products to our trading partners instead of dollars to balance our trade obligations? Why not offer them oil and gas as well? I think that would be a win-win.

Since the 1960s, the purchasing power of the dollar has been reduced by a factor of 10. At the time, depending on where you lived, a nice house could be purchased for somewhere between $15,000 and $25,000. A nice new car cost $3,000. A good income was $10,000, and a great income was $20,000. A gallon of gasoline cost a mere 25 cents. Multiply all these by ten and you have the present situation.

Technology, Longevity, Economy, Liberty

The inflation situation in some European countries has been even worse throughout the 20th century. In France, for instance, the franc lost so much value that it was replaced by the NEW franc, equal to 100 OLD francs. Maybe we should follow that lead and create a NEW dollar equal to ten OLD dollars. Perhaps then, prices in NEW dollars would emulate prices in OLD dollars 50 years ago. Having a million (NEW) dollars would, once again, be rare and prices would not seem so outlandishly high. Maybe we could revive our gold standard with an ounce of gold worth somewhere around 100 NEW dollars. Even if we leave our currency alone, the reforms I propose could possibly create more prosperity and, yes, even make us proud once again to be Americans.

Surely there is a way to harness the advantages we have as a nation to enhance the well-being of our least fortunate while, simultaneously, improving the lives of those around the world who should be the natural beneficiaries of a true global economy. There must be a way to utilize the enhanced productivity of technology to improve the lot of ordinary people without their being forced to become totally dependent upon the state for their support. And, certainly, there is a way for ordinary people to accumulate enough wealth during their working years to live out their years beyond retirement securely and with as little public support as possible. I have written this book to address my fear of ordinary people returning to their former position as chattel for the privileged—loss of liberty—if nothing changes.

Closing Arguments

REFERENCES

1. About News, useconomy.about.com

2. Reported by Jim Geraghty in National Review May 15, 2015

3. Originally printed in the Los Angeles Times. Read in "The Moral Case for Fossil Fuels' by Alex Epstein

4. New York Times May 30, 2015

5. Dr. Aubrey De Gray pronouncement reported in numerous publications February 2011.

6. Wikipedia "Battle of Hampton Roads"

7. "Is Liberalism Dead" in "Shattered Consensus" James Piereson

8. "Race, Politics and Lies" Thomas Sowell Jewish World Review May 15, 2015

9. "The Keynesian Revolution" in "Shattered Consensus" James Piereson

10. David Stockman "The Great Deformation"

APPENDIX 1
TACKLING THE DEBT

My methodology for examining our bloated debt and proposing a method to eliminate it over time, discussed in Chapter 12, is based on many assumptions, and, therefore may be somewhat flawed. But, most economists rely on all sorts of assumptions to come up with their models. In that regard, I am no exception, except that most of them have access to data I do not have and have produced models that predict second and third order effects of government actions. For example, a decrease of Social Security benefits might have an impact on gross spending and, therefore, affect the Gross Domestic Product (GDP) negatively. However, such data may or may not be relevant to the task at hand, if, for example, the drop in spending is more than compensated for by increased confidence that Medicare fraud and abuse is being addressed and corrected. Or that the annual deficits are being reduced, leading to greater confidence by well off retirees that future inflation is being reduced or eliminated, so they will spend more of their retirement income with less anxiety. No economic model out there can adjust for these perceptions in advance.

Therefore, I do not apologize for ignoring these real world consequences in my analysis. What I basically did was to assume a long term 2% average increase in GDP which, if anything, is likely to be lower than actual over the time frame discussed. That makes my analysis less optimistic than is likely, and a long term debt reduction plan may be even easier to achieve than I have predicted. Also, I have assumed that the 2% increase in GDP each year would result precisely in a revenue increase of exactly that. The model I used assumes that revenue would remain at 17.2% of GDP, which is a reasonable average over the past two decades or so.

I personally believe, unlike most Republicans or other conservatives, that the tax code should be modified to equilibrate the tax on dividends and capital gains. That would encourage more investors to demand their share of the companies' profits they invest in on an annual basis in the form of dividends as this would eliminate the capital gains tax advantage inherent in selling a portion of those securities as a means of profit taking. That would make the stock market more prone to having CEO's obtain shareholders' permission to reinvest instead of distributing earnings without their

Appendices

consent. This would make the markets less volatile and, therefore, their investors far more secure.

I also assumed that interest rate will remain steady. That is perhaps my worst assumption but I do not know how to make a better guess. My sense is that interest rates will remain low, particularly if a sincere effort is made to rein in government spending, because it will decrease the overall demand for capital. I do not expect rates to go up very rapidly if sovereign demand across the globe is reduced.

My main consideration here is to conceive of a debt reduction scenario that involves some pain but is viewed as fair. I believe that entitlement spending needs to be reined in a bit with cuts falling most heavily on the most affluent groups and not at all on the least. I also believe that a modest tax increase on the most affluent may be justified without harming the economy but I did not include this in my calculations. I believe that corporate taxes need to be reduced to make US based industry more competitive but that individual taxes should be increased on the most affluent to make up that shortfall. In that I agree with the Democrats. What I have a problem with is Democrat talk that the deficit can be completely eliminated by taxing the rich. That is a fiction and they know it. Class warfare is no substitute for intelligent governance. In true welfare state countries such as Denmark the government burden is about 50% of the GDP. If Democrats want Americans to buy into such a system, fine, but do not lie and tell the people it can be accomplished with no impact on taxation for ordinary people.

My plan assumes that non entitlement government spending will be reduced by about 17% over ten years and that average entitlement spending will be reduced by an *average* of 7% *per person* over ten years with the biggest burden falling on the most affluent, and none falling on the least affluent. Note that I have taken into account that the population of Social Security and Medicare recipients will increase year by year. I hope that ways will be found to reduce improper Medicare spending and fraud in particular and suspect that that alone will accomplish the reductions we should be seeking.

Something needs to be said about my subsequent proposal in Chapter 13 concerning transforming Social Security into a private savings vehicle for making retirement far more secure and prosperous for just about all workers. Regardless of their political party, nearly everyone believes that the Social Security system is improperly funded and needs to be transformed. Beliefs on how it should be transformed splits pretty evenly along party lines with Democrats firmly opposed to privatization and Republicans firmly in line.

The principal opposition by Democrats is the extreme volatility of the equities markets. I strongly agree with Democrats on that point and argue for regulations (Chapter 14) that would greatly diminish wild fluctuations in market valuations caused by leveraged speculation based on rumors about actions of the Fed that have no bearing on any company's core value. Only if those regulations come to pass would I favor privatization though I believe that even with today's wild fluctuations private accounts would serve the population better than today's system.

My long term theory for tackling loss of jobs to automation is to find a way for workers to eventually own

Appendices

a fair share of the equity capital of the country so that they develop a cash flow from that equity that replaces wages. This will take at least one generation to accomplish. President Reagan initiated the IRA system which was a great start but it conferred too much undeserved power to Wall Street firms who, unfortunately, abused their implied fiduciary responsibility by creating volatile markets with unprecedented leveraged trading that created a system of boom and bust over the last 30 or so years. That has to come to an end. Once it is, the stock market can become a secure vehicle for income first for retirees and then for their heirs as a substitute for wages as industry after industry roll back their payrolls.

One major obstacle with privatization is that today's Social Security system is basically a Ponzi scheme. Today's recipients do not receive the funds they contributed. That money has already been spent. Instead, money collected from present workers is used to pay present retirees. Therefore, if privatization goes into effect it will have the effect of temporarily increasing federal spending to cover the cost of present recipients. My plan would be to phase privatization in over 45 years or so. For the individual who is only one year from retirement, that individual would receive 44/45ths of his Social Security payment along with his one year of privatization. For someone two years away, he would receive 43/45ths of his Social Security payment plus two years of privatization and so on. So, over time, the government cost of Social Security will diminish.

Initially, the cost of government will increase to make up for the fact that payroll taxes that presently finance Social

Security benefits will disappear. But, over time, the government obligation to pay out Social Security benefits will also slowly disappear, but not Medicare payments that will continue and be financed by payroll deductions. The net effect will be nearly neutral and the national debt will disappear in roughly the same time frame, around 35 years. A summary of what can be done with to eliminate our national debt even if we privatize Social Security but reduce expenditures as previously described appears below:

CALCULATION OF NATIONAL DEBT 2015-2050 ($ TRILLION)
PRIVATIZATION OF SOCIAL SECURITY

	2015	2020	2030	2040	2050
BUDGET	3.7	3.6	3.6	3.5	3.6
RECEIPTS	2.4	2.7	3.6	4.9	6.5
DEFICIT/(SURPLUS)	1.3	0.9	(0.1)	(1.4)	(3.2)
NATIONAL DEBT	19.4	21.3	20.0	13.8	0.7

The numbers presented here and in Chapter 12 were worked out on a fairly extensive examination of demographic factors and assumptions about longevity and birth rates. I made conservative assumptions. For longevity, I assumed that over the next 35 years, life expectancy would increase to 90 years. I also assumed that birth rates would neither increase nor decline so that the work force remains constant. I probably should have added people to the work force to account for the reduction of able bodied people living on welfare or disability benefits, but that would only have made my calculations more optimistic. So, for all intents and purposes, my calculations

Appendices

represent the near worst case scenario for the economic recovery from where we are today to where we could be with some belt tightening, without hurting the most vulnerable.

I have put a lot of time and effort into building reasonable economic models for the cases I describe. If a reader wishes me to provide new predictions based on their assumptions, I will be happy to provide those results. Please e-mail me at bob.ennis@juno.com with the case you wish to see and I will work it out and send you the results.

APPENDIX 2
TACKLING THE TRADE DEFICIT

There is a great deal of difference between the fair trade we have with high wage countries like Germany and the very unfair trade we have with low wage countries, particularly China. Our trade with Germany is dominated with German companies such as Mercedes or BMW. Over the past forty years or so, German currency has achieved parity with the US dollar. In the early 1970's the deutschmark traded at about $0.25, and increased steadily since then so that German wages (now in Euros) are at par with American wages in dollars. As a result it became more economic for the German firms BMW and Mercedes to build plants in the US for many of the models they sell here. Such trade benefits US workers as well as German workers as long as the trading terms are similar; that is that the import taxes for German products coming into the US are similar for US products coming into Germany.

While we have a negative balance of trade with Germany, I still consider this trade to be fair. I believe, however, that it could and should be improved and perhaps will be improved in the near future. Even though Mercedes' and BMW's are assembled here, most, if not all, components are still produced overseas and contribute to our negative balance with Germany.

Our greatest opportunity to improve our trade balance with Germany is to develop our liquefied natural gas (LNG) export industry. I am also perplexed why we do not insist on requiring German cars that are assembled here, to at least have steel body parts (fenders, bumpers, hoods, etc.) produced here. These commodity type items should surely be able to be produced here without disturbing the economics of the manufacturing processes for these companies and would be a huge help to our faltering steel industry. However, even if that is done, it is improbable that such production would help many displaced workers in the "rust belt'. The beneficiaries would be workers in southern states like Kentucky that were not associated with auto workers' or steel workers' unions that drove prices up so high and quality so low that it invited the German (and Japanese) invasion.

Our trade with China and other low wage countries (including even Mexico) is entirely different and rests on the fallacy that it is free and fair. The principal and fundamental difference is that such trade is based almost entirely on US companies abandoning their facilities in the US and repositioning them in those countries. It is not Toyota or

Appendices

Mercedes that we are trading with. It is Apple, Microsoft, Motorola and others. Products made by these fundamentally American companies have taken their manufacturing abroad but still rely on the US market for the lion's share of its profits. That is fundamentally unfair, to both US workers and workers in these low wage countries.

Furthermore, it has created a structural deficiency in our economy. Displaced workers do not have the means to purchase these products, even if they are cheaper than they would be if they were made in the US. As a result, these unfortunates must find ways to survive. They take on short lived jobs in the underground economy, like painting houses for the more affluent among us. I have hired several to do work for me. They probably pay no taxes, and, in addition they obtain welfare payments from the government and free (but poor quality) medical care by going to emergency rooms in hospitals that must take care of them.

In theory, such loss of employment here should create deflation so that wages in dollars here achieve parity with those of low wage countries. But that would be a disaster for the banking industry as borrowers would have to pay back loans with dollars that are worth far more than their value when borrowed. Banks (and their borrowers) prefer inflation so that the paid back dollars are worth less than the dollars they borrowed. Workers, by expecting annual wage increases, without corresponding productivity increases, also create inflation. No worker would stand still for having his wages decreased annually in a deflationary environment even if those reduced wages purchased more goods this year than the previous year. So, we have the fiction of higher wages year after year with no net real income gain. This has been going on for most of the period since Nixon let the dollar float and abandoned the gold standard.

Since then the percentage of working age people actually working in the work force has declined dramatically. Some are in the underground economy, earning untaxed income in addition to their government stipends. Many have succeeded in getting themselves classified as disabled and collect money allocated for that purpose from the Social Security Trust Fund.

The Federal Reserve finances this state of affairs by buying Treasury Bills needed to finance such largesse and other forms of welfare as well as retirement benefits and medical payment for retirees. By so doing, they foster sufficient inflation to avoid the dreaded scenario of constantly reduced prices for goods and services that would occur in a truly free market economy. Absent such intervention, prices would drop, dollars would become more valuable, and wages would approach equilibrium with the low wage countries to which US manufacturers have fled.

The distortion inherent in propping up US prices because countries like China have not allowed their currencies to increase dramatically against the dollar - in the way that the German deutschmark, Swiss franc, or Japanese yen have—is the fundamental reason I consider our trade with low wage countries, principally China, as inherently different from real free trade and why I part company with many on the right who view such trade as perfectly acceptable even as they rail at the Fed for financing our bloated debt. What should the

Appendices

Fed do? Allow these unfortunates to starve to death in front of our eyes? I say to them, "connect the dots." You are so quick to blame those on the left for not seeing connections that are obvious to you because of a blind spot caused by their ideology. Do not be guilty of your own blind spots.

My potential solutions for creating a fair and balanced trade with low wage countries become murky because, by and large, it is the American companies who move their manufacturing to such havens who hold the money in those countries and they cannot repatriate those dollars to the US without sustaining the US tax rate for those dollars. So, say they have a billion dollar profit after paying tax where the product has been manufactured, if they wish to reinvest that money in the US they would first have to pay $450 million in tax. That is a huge disincentive for that company to reinvest in the US and, as a result, only dividends to US shareholders get back into the country. These shareholders pay tax on the dividends they receive but they pay that tax independent of where the product is manufactured. So, to a shareholder, it makes no difference where the product is made. In fact, for the shareholder, it is almost certainly better for the product to be made in a low wage country and sold in a high wage country because the profit margin for that country is greater. Hence, there is a booming stock market here while wages here are stagnant and more people drop permanently out of the work force every year. This scenario has been going on for forty or more years.

Now consider that a worker is, perhaps, several times more likely to lose his job to automation as to a low wage country.

Technology, Longevity, Economy, Liberty

Just today, Monday, December 05, 2016 I hear on TV that Amazon is designing a system that would eliminate cashiers in supermarkets. This follows elimination of some order takers in fast food establishments such as Sheetz in Pennsylvania. This technological reduction of labor has been going on at a snail's pace for several decades; consider toll booths for example. First we had baskets to collect tolls and we now have EZ Pass and other systems to allow motorists to coast through toll booths with their installed transponder handling the transaction. Also consider ATM machines. In the future there will be driverless delivery trucks and taxis, and soon we will have remote robotically controlled "you name it."

Therefore, the idea of 'work', particularly the low skilled variety, but constantly replacing more and more sophisticated employment, needs to be addressed. The path ahead for employment as we know it is diminishing rapidly, as opposed to opportunity in the private sector particularly for knowledge based improvements that provide intellectual property for the creator or for other more normal small business service enterprises. We need entirely new thinking about the economic contract between ordinary citizens and society as a whole. To my way of thinking, the challenge is to create a society where many more people will earn large chunks of their living as entrepreneurs or as shareholders. As I have stated elsewhere in numerous places, I believe privatization of the Social Security system can go a long way toward realizing that goal. But it will take a full generation to accomplish.

Appendices

APPENDIX 3
TAMING THE STOCK MARKET

I regard the taming of the stock market as a high priority function if we are ever able to defeat the triple whammy that has changed the contract between citizens and the overall economy. We have come to a point in human history that can visualize the end of labor as a significant economic variable. At the same time, as people are living into their 90's and beyond at record rates, even if they had successful stints as employees or self-employed service providers, they will be required to use their accumulated wealth to finance those late years in their life or be forced to accept some form of welfare or other government largesse.

To my way of thinking, the challenge is to create a society where many more people will earn large chunks of their living as entrepreneurs or as shareholders. I think that privatization of the Social Security system can go a long way toward realizing that goal. My thoughts on that issue are explained in Chapter 13 as well as Appendix 1. If we are ever to accomplish that goal, it will be necessary for people to trust the stock market to be far freer of booms and busts than it is at the present.

If the markets are to be tamed, the reasons for these wide fluctuations need to be examined. Substantial participation in the stock market was originally limited to only the most affluent members of society. That changed dramatically in the 80's as many companies began opting out of providing pensions for their retired workforce. This followed the economic turmoil of the 70's during which time the country experienced unprecedented inflation and loss of jobs that, more or less, put an end to the concept of long term employment for much of the population.

The stock market crash of 1929 was a wake-up call to the country to rein in excess stock market speculation. Laws were enacted to accomplish precisely that. Notably, the markets were limited to borrowing no more than 50% of the value of a portfolio. If stocks dropped to below 50% of that value, the owner was obliged to come up with enough cash to cover the shortfall. That regulation kept the markets relatively stable from the 30's onward, but in the 80's as more and more money flowed into the markets, sharp traders saw the economic windfall that could occur if owners could control stock values with as low as, say, 10% of the face value of the stock in question. The concept of the stock option was born.

The option concept was a clear dodge around the 50% rule in place since the 30's but the market was on a roll as

Appendices

more and more money kept pouring in, so many people were enriched and caution was thrown to the wind. Then, in October 1987, the market collapsed as stocks plummeted by 30% or more in a single day. But it didn't stay down for very long because the Federal Reserve intervened in a way it had never done before. And, I must say, there was a very good reason for such intervention. By 1987 the market had become the store of wealth needed by common people to finance their retirements as fixed pensions had begun to disappear. So Mr. Greenspan, the Fed's Chairman at the time panicked and did measures designed to prop up prices on the stock markets. He started reducing interest rates.

As rates on bonds decreased, the return on stocks also decreased as reflected by higher and higher price-to-earnings (PE) ratio. Historically PE ratios for blue chip stocks ran at about 13 or 14 to 1, reflecting about 7% to 7½% return. But over the 90's Greenspan manipulated interest rates downward so that by the end of the decade PE ratios had risen to 30, reflecting a return of only about 3.3% on stocks. Throughout that period stock prices were rising as they never had never risen before, but the rise was phony as it was not based on earnings but only based on higher valuations reflecting a lower, not higher, rate of return. Something had to give and it did. Stock prices were now prone to periodic crashes as bubble after bubble burst. And each time it burst, the Fed did everything in its power to keep the party rolling, primarily by lowering interest rates even further as a means of propping up market valuations so as not to panic all the new stock market investors who were saving for retirement in their IRA's and 401K's.

Technology, Longevity, Economy, Liberty

Meanwhile the major investment banking houses were developing even greater ways to leverage their funds in the markets. With derivatives they were able to control vast amounts of shares with truly ridiculously low amounts of their own capital. Leverage rates of 60 or 80 times became possible and this new class of robber barons started buying up industry after industry by monetizing the assets of the companies they wished to take over by issuing highly rated bonds at ridiculously low interest rates, thanks to the Fed continuously pushing interest rates downward, while, all the while keeping stock valuations sky high. In company after company, they stripped the assets, made large profits selling their stock and left the companies they invaded with massive debt, more than many could ever hope to pay back. For a thorough analysis of how this was done and who did it, I recommend David Stockman's book *The Great Deformation* to my readers.

By the time of the Great Recession of 2008, interest rates had been brought down to nearly zero. The way I see things, nothing much has improved since then as stock prices are continuing to escalate far more rapidly than their earnings can justify. In fact, once again according to Stockman, earnings have not budged since then but stock prices have advanced mightily. This suggests that we are soon in for another crash.

The only way to solve this problem is to do away with the high degree of leverage taking place in the markets by banning options and derivatives and going back to sensible regulations put into effect in the 1930's to limit stock accounts to only very low limits of leverage. Once that is done and interest rates revert to market driven values, we will, as Stockman says, have

Appendices

the means to have "price discovery". That is interest rates on bonds and bank accounts reflecting supply and demand and the same for stock valuations. When that day comes around, I would be a great advocate for privatizing Social Security, making it the vehicle by which ordinary individuals attain their rightful share in the overall economy. This is necessary as automation, globalization and longevity have made the need for ownership to replace labor as the means for normal everyday people to live well and prosper. Without it, it will be necessary for the large majority of ordinary people to become wards of the state and take whatever the state decides to give.

www.ingramcontent.com/pod-product-compliance
Lightning Source LLC
Chambersburg PA
CBHW060838170526
45158CB00001B/183